D0405779

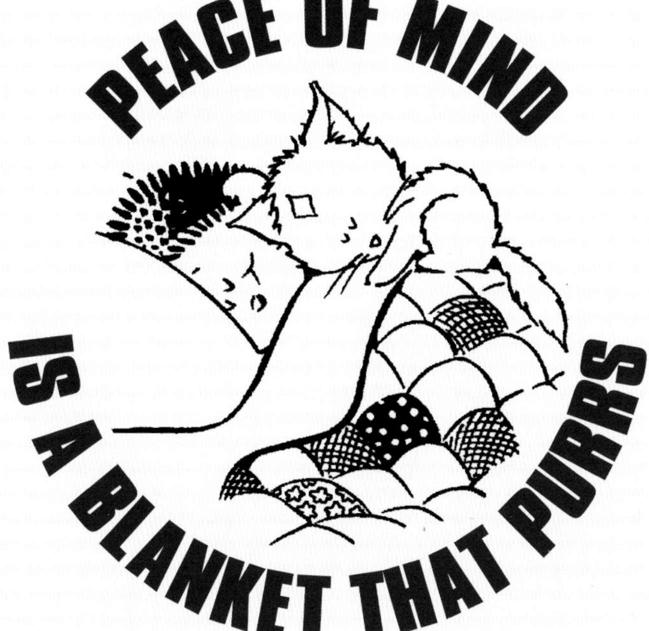
PEACE OF MIND
IS A BLANKET THAT PURRS

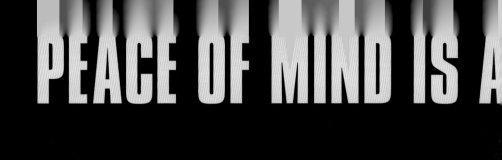

PEACE OF MIND IS A

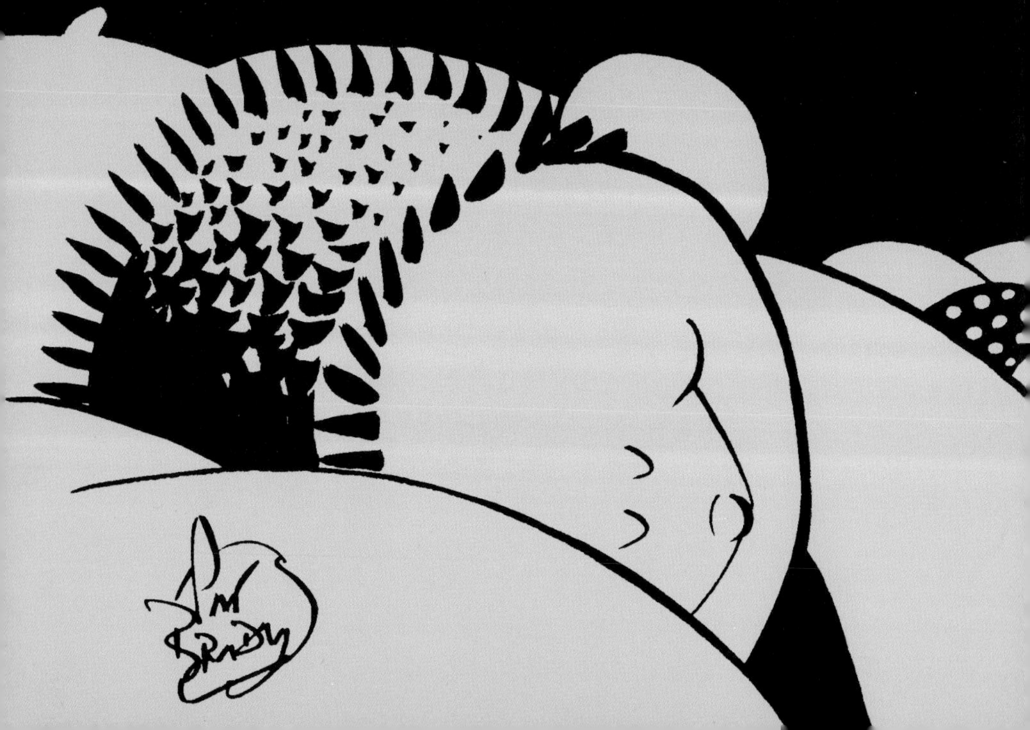

BLANKET THAT PURRS

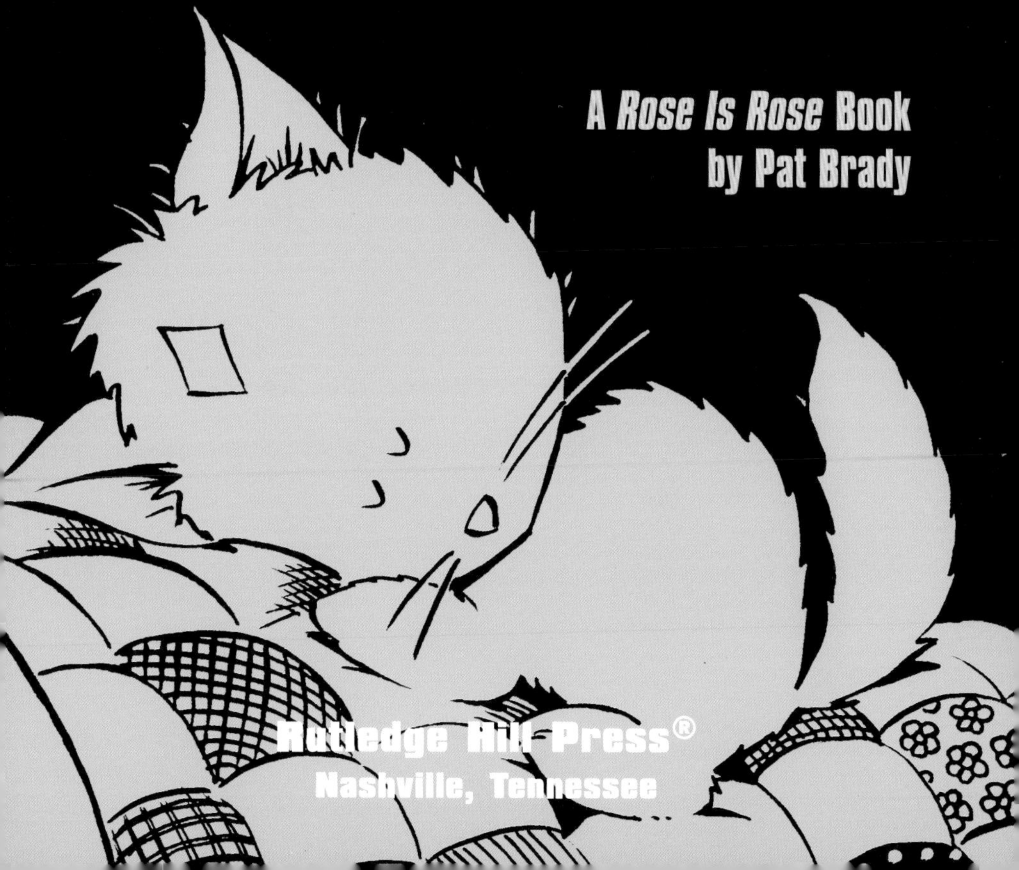

A *Rose Is Rose* Book
by Pat Brady

Rutledge Hill Press®
Nashville, Tennessee

Published in Nashville, Tennessee, by Rutledge Hill Press®, Inc., 211 Seventh Avenue North, Nashville, Tennessee 37219. Distributed in Canada by H. B. Fenn & Company, Ltd., 34 Nixon Road, Bolton, Ontario L7E 1W2. Distributed in Australia by The Five Mile Press Pty., Ltd., 22 Summit Road, Noble Park, Victoria 3174. Distributed in New Zealand by Tandem Press, 2 Rugby Road, Birkenhead, Auckland 10. Distributed in the United Kingdom by Verulam Publishing, Ltd., 152a Park Street Lane, Park Street, St. Albans, Hertfordshire AL2 2AU.

Library of Congress Cataloging in Publication Data is available.
ISBN 1-55853-615-9

Printed in China

1 2 3 4 5 6 7 8 9 — 03 02 01 00 99 98

Typography & graphics assemblage by Ernie Couch / Consultx

PEACE OF MIND IS A BLANKET THAT PURRS

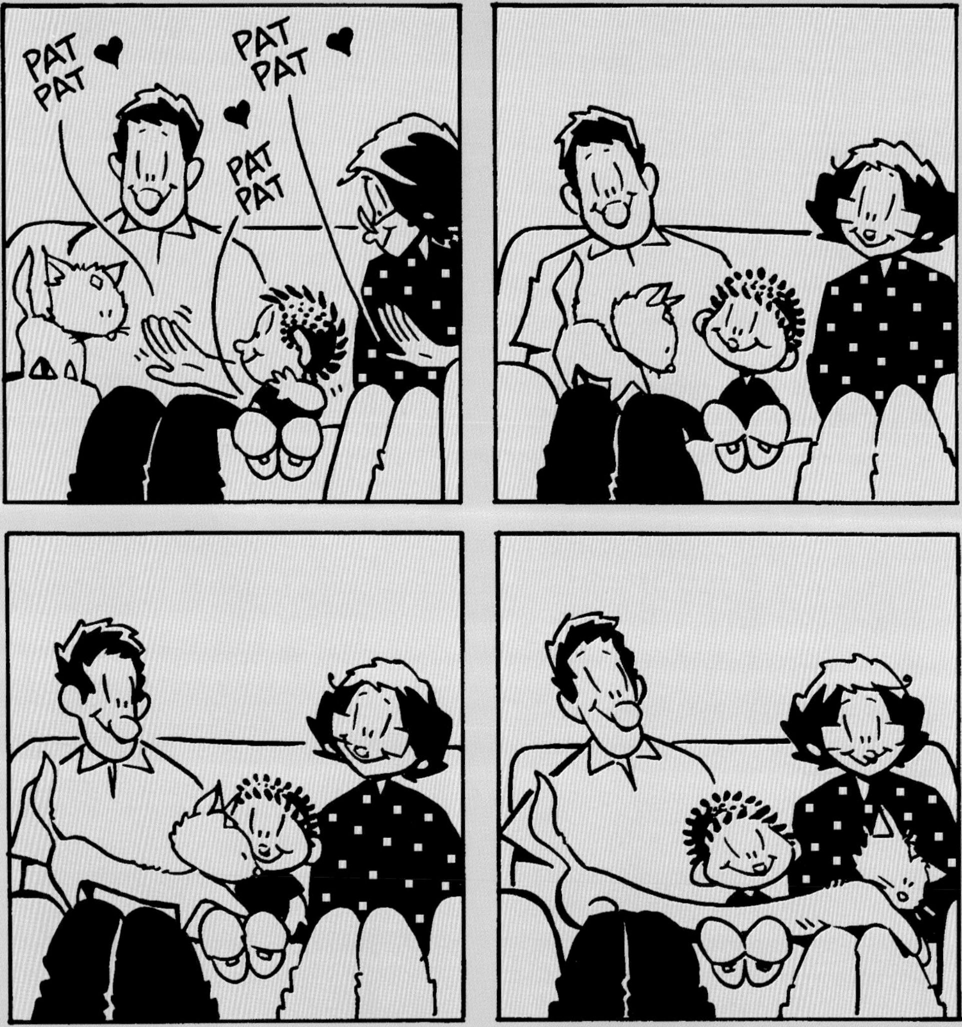
PAT
PAT
PAT
PAT
PAT
PAT

PEACE OF MIND

IS HAVING

PLENTY

OF

LAPS

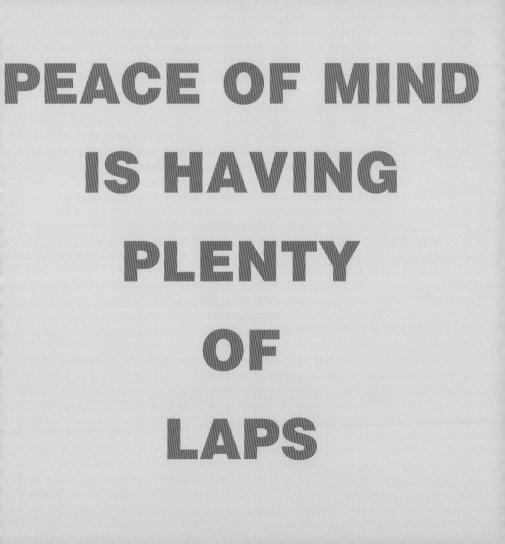

PEACE OF MIND IS HEARING YOUR PARENT'

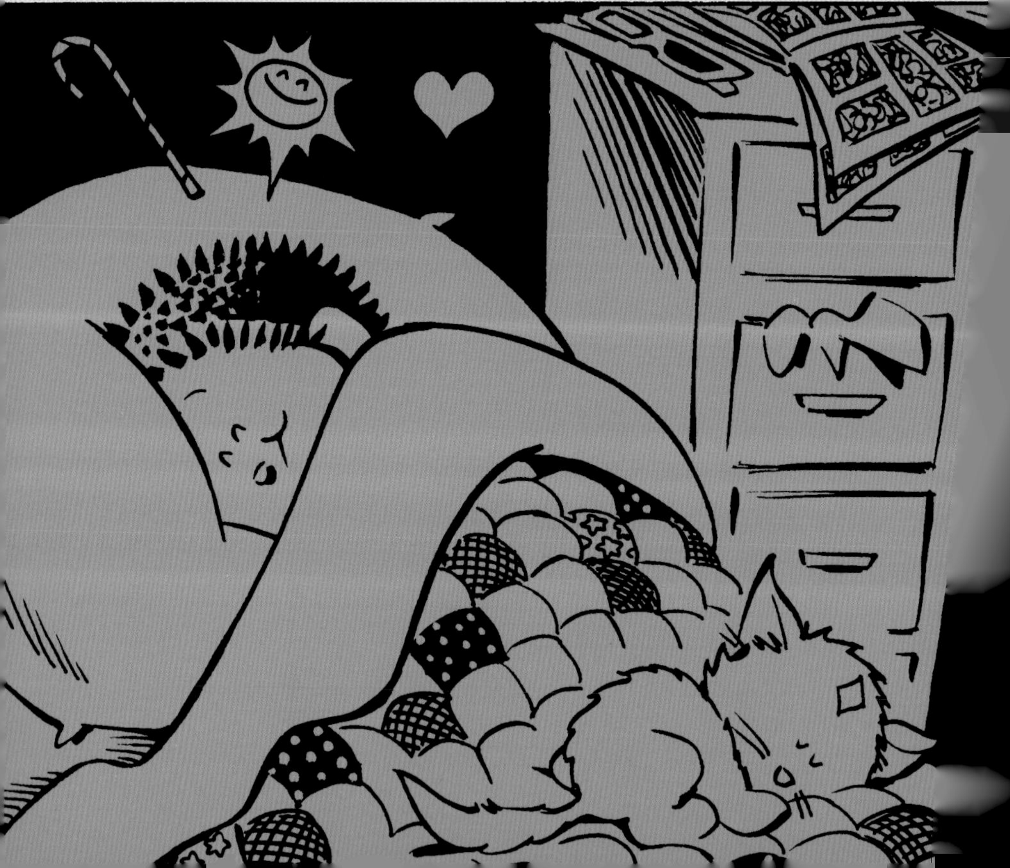

HING OUT LOUD IN THE KITCHEN

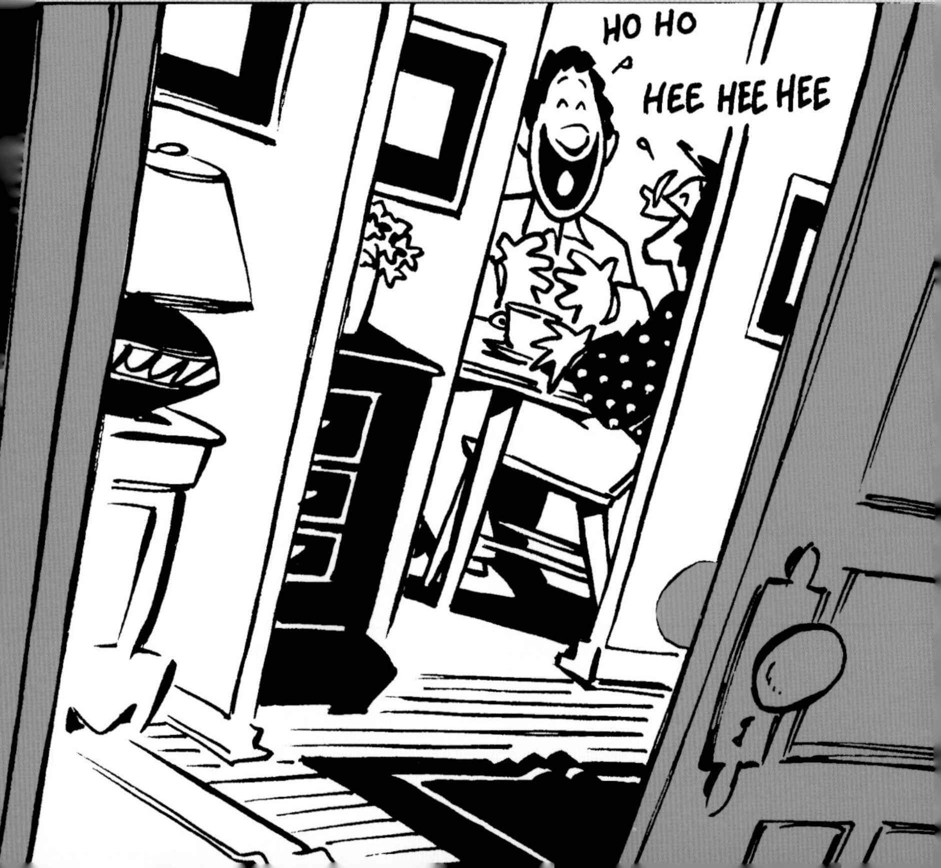
HO HO
HEE HEE HEE

PEACE OF MIND IS PAJAMAS STILL WARM FROM THE DRYER

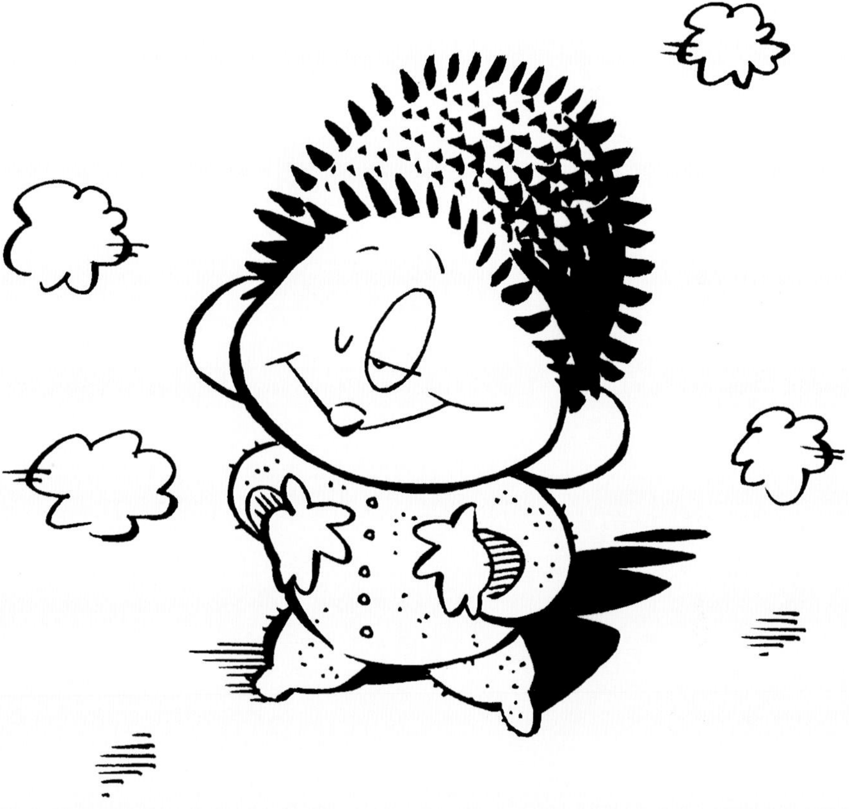

PEACE OF MIND IS A "THUMBS-UP"

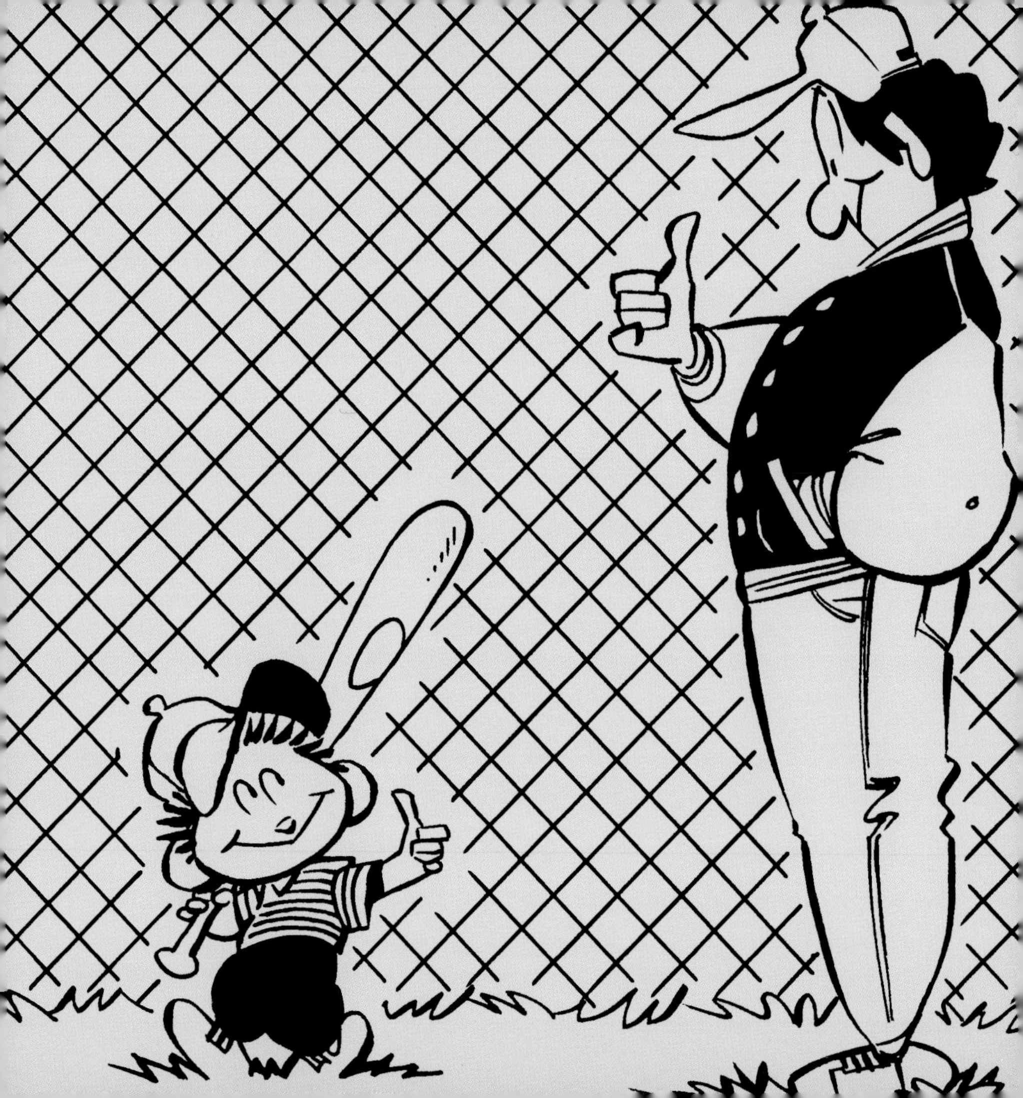

PEACE OF MIND IS KNOWING HOW TO FIND YOUR CLASSROOM

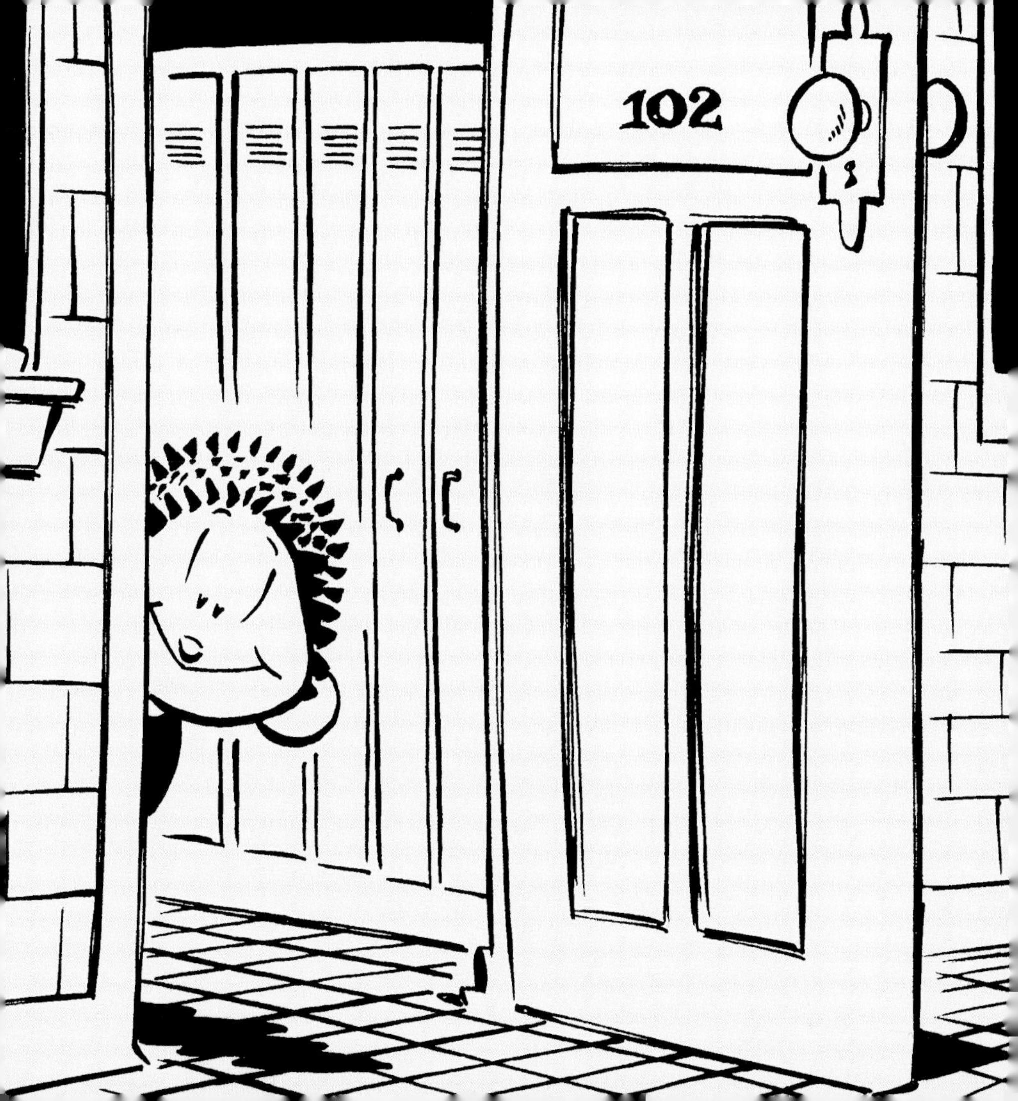
102

Peace of Mind
is
having
someone
say,
"be careful"

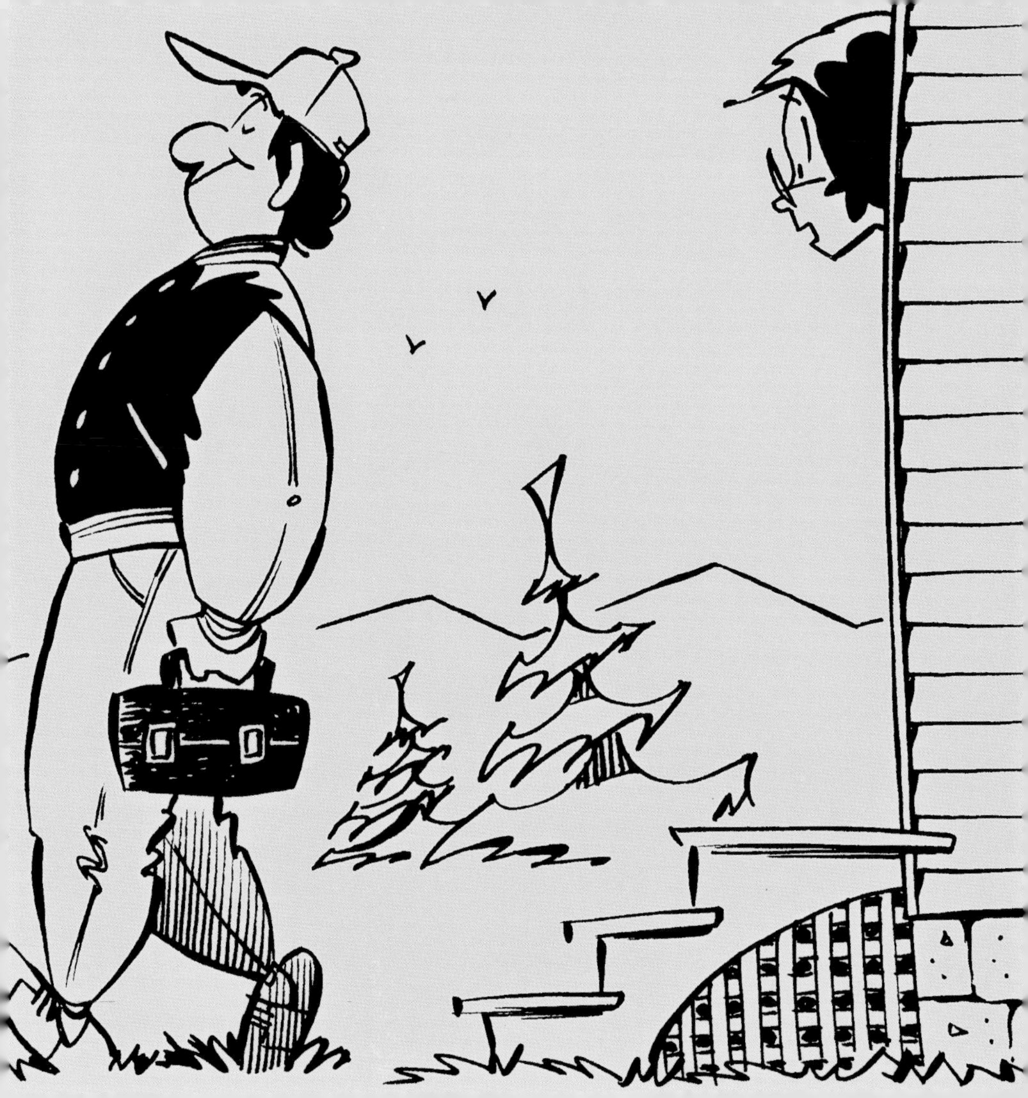

PEACE OF MIND IS A GOOD STRETCH

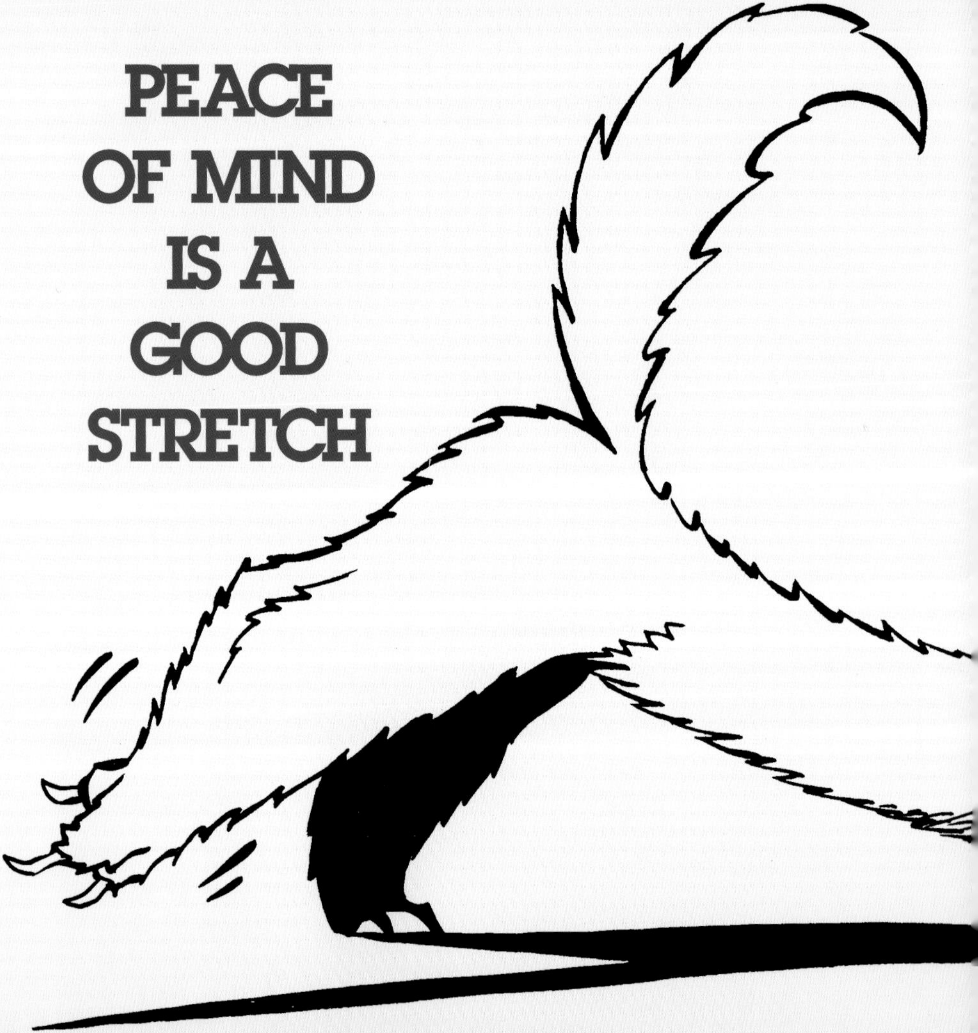

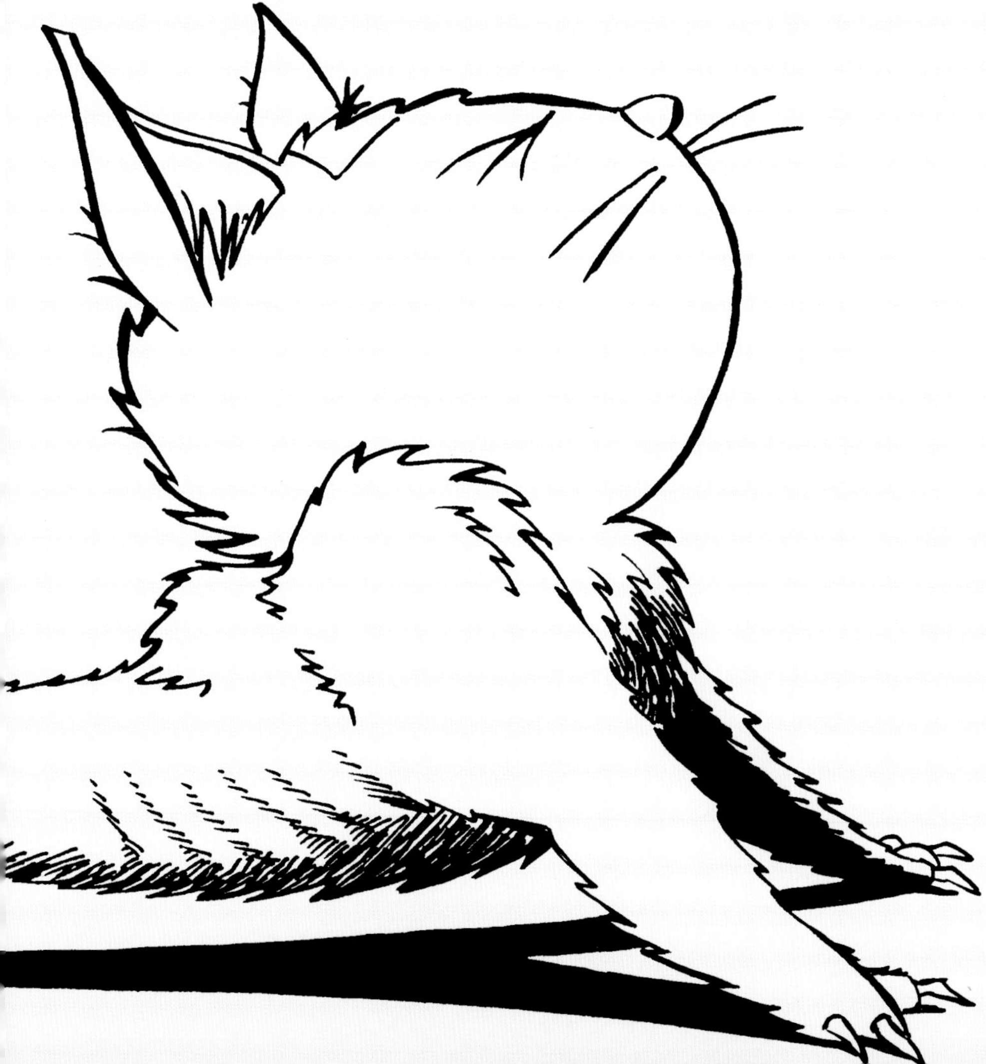

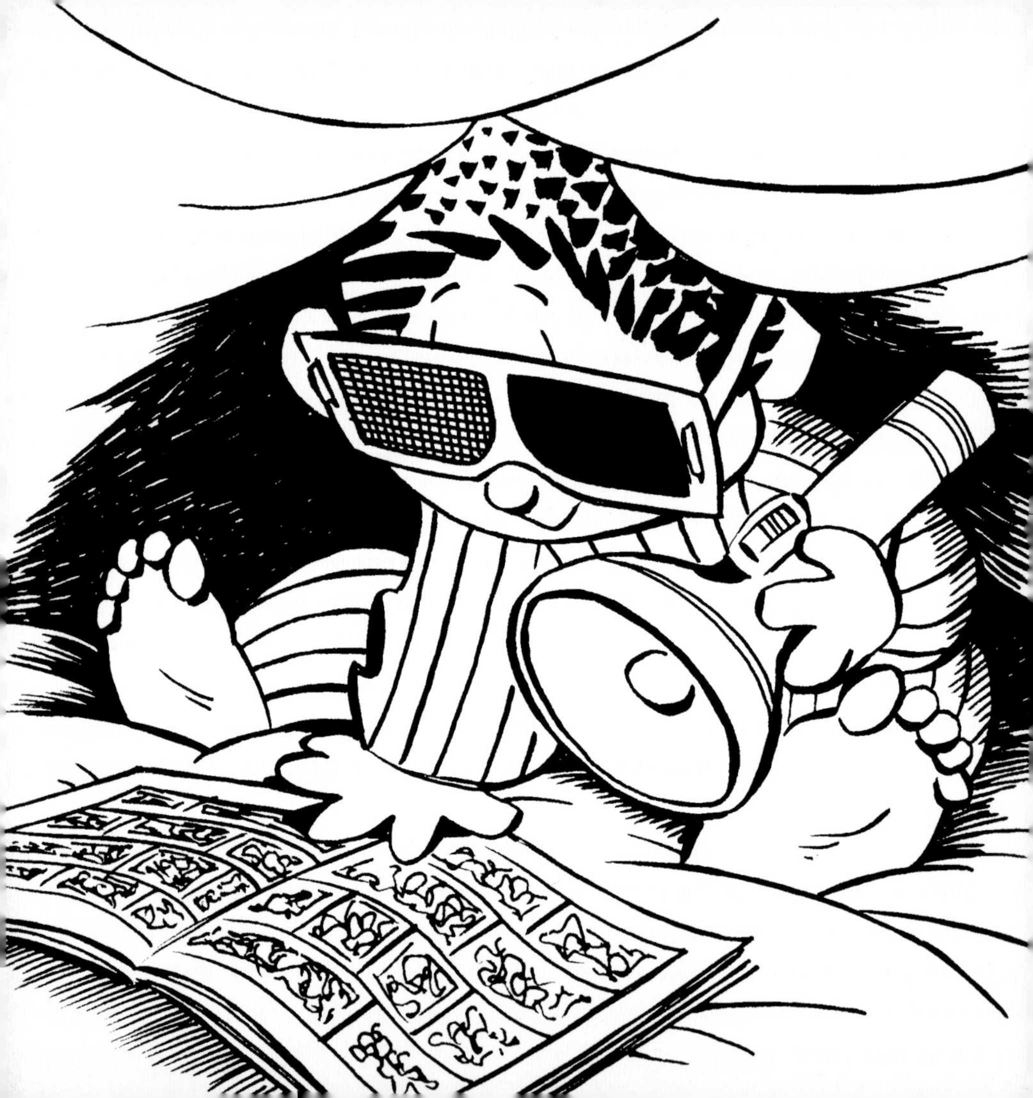

PEACE OF MIND IS A BED SHEET TENT, A FLASHLIGHT AND A 3-D COMIC

PEACE OF MIND IS HEARING THE WORDS, "I'M HOME!"

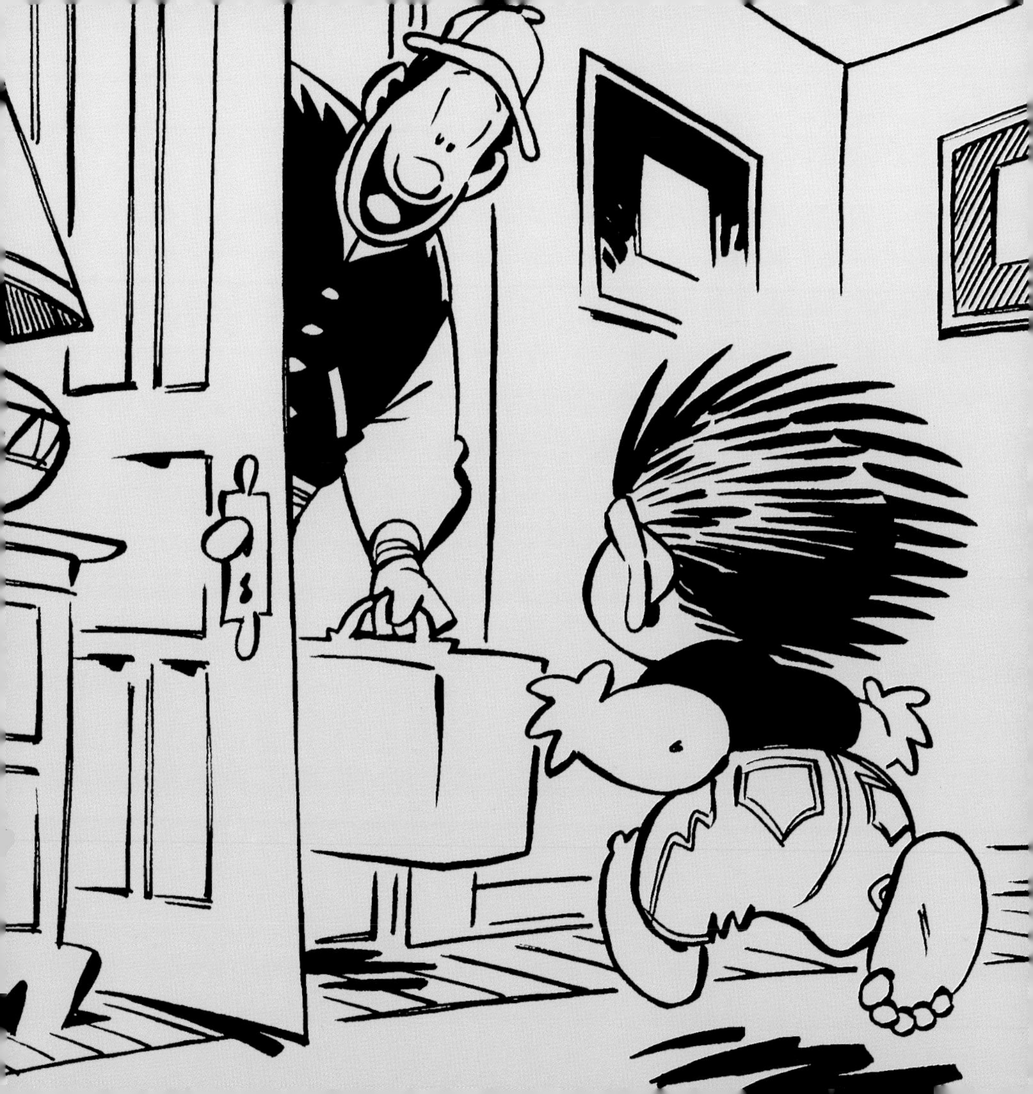

PEACE OF MIND IS KNOWING WHERE YOU CAME FROM

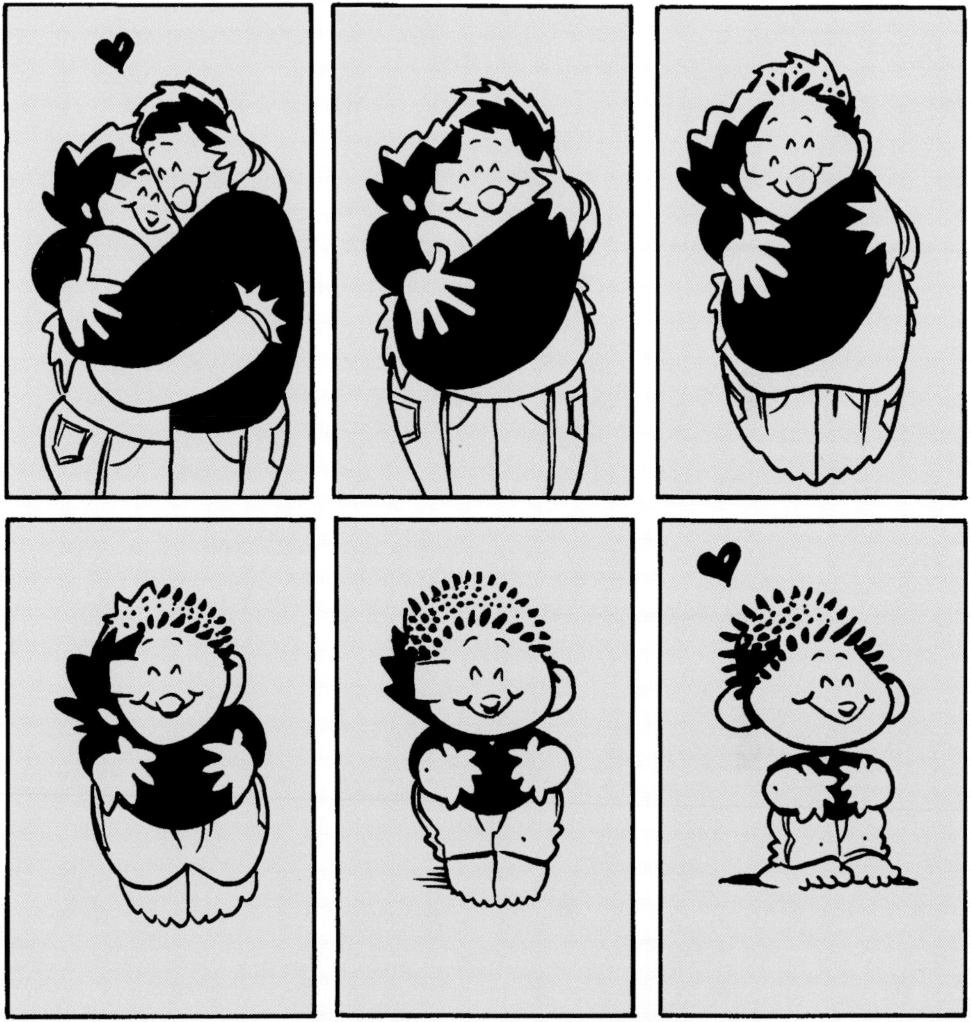

PEACE OF MIND IS

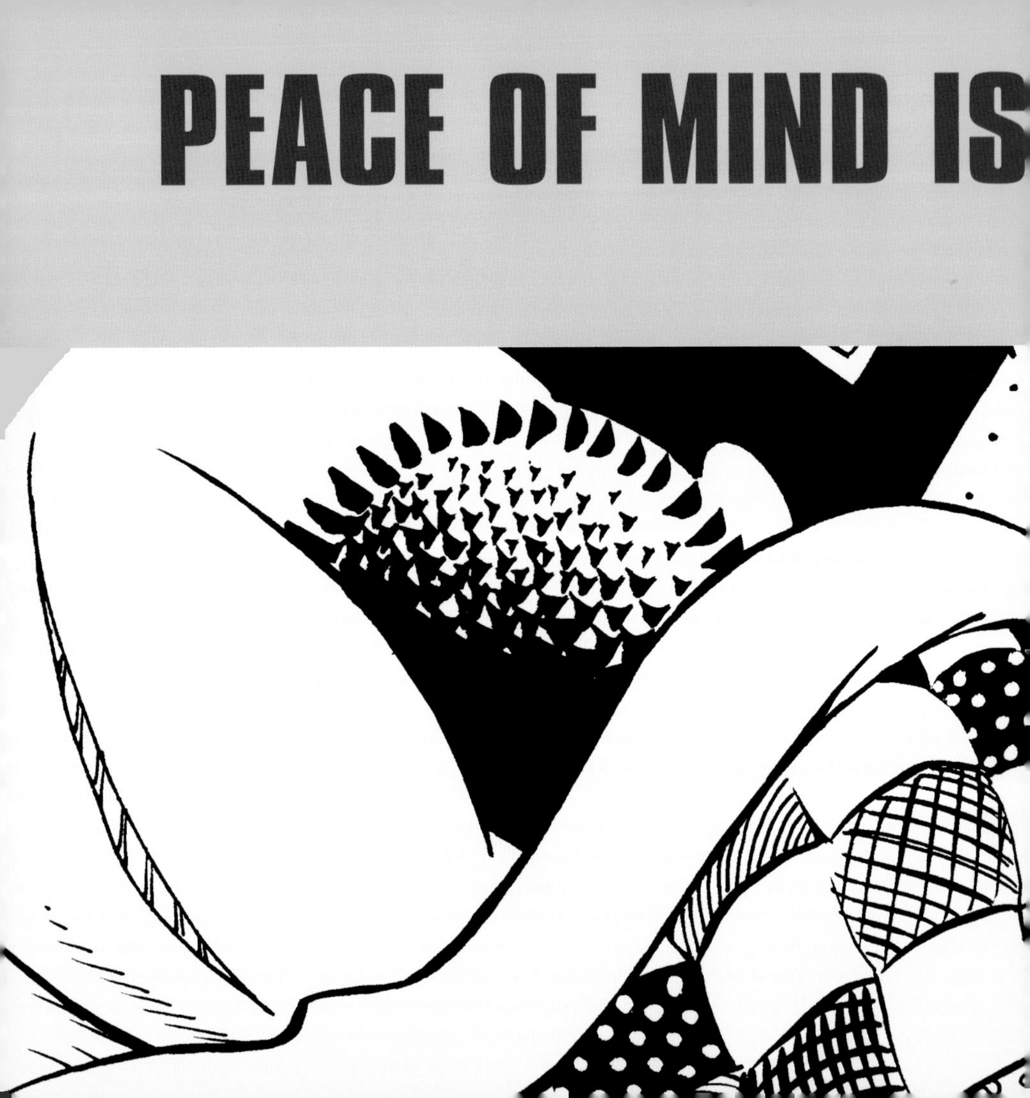

A SUNRISE WITH FUR

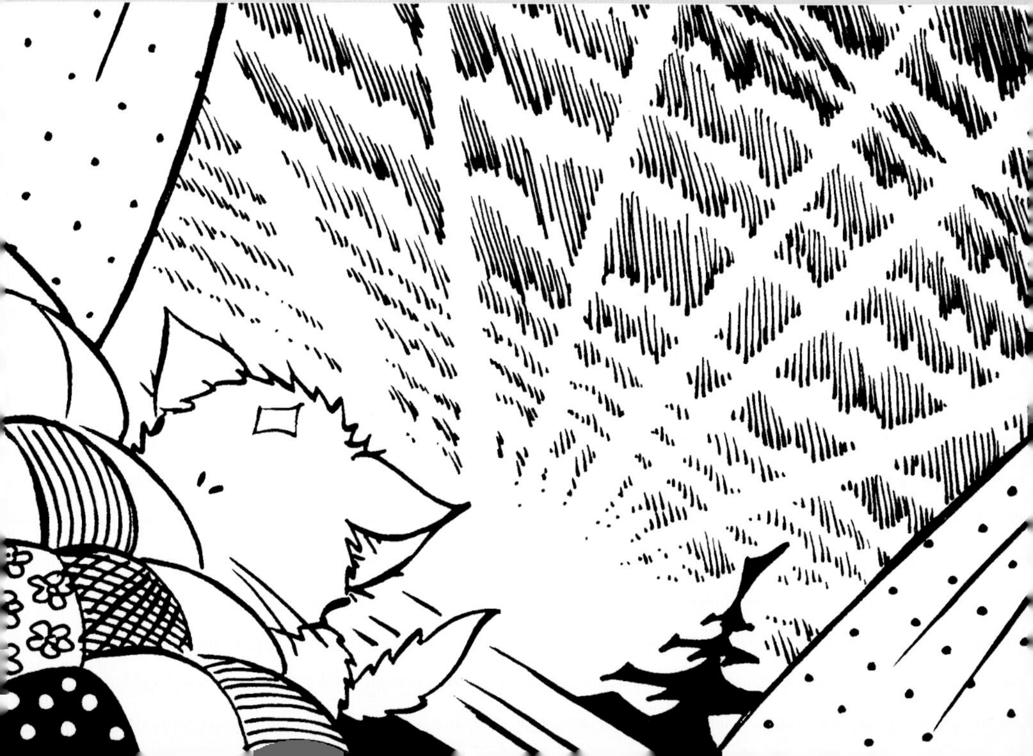

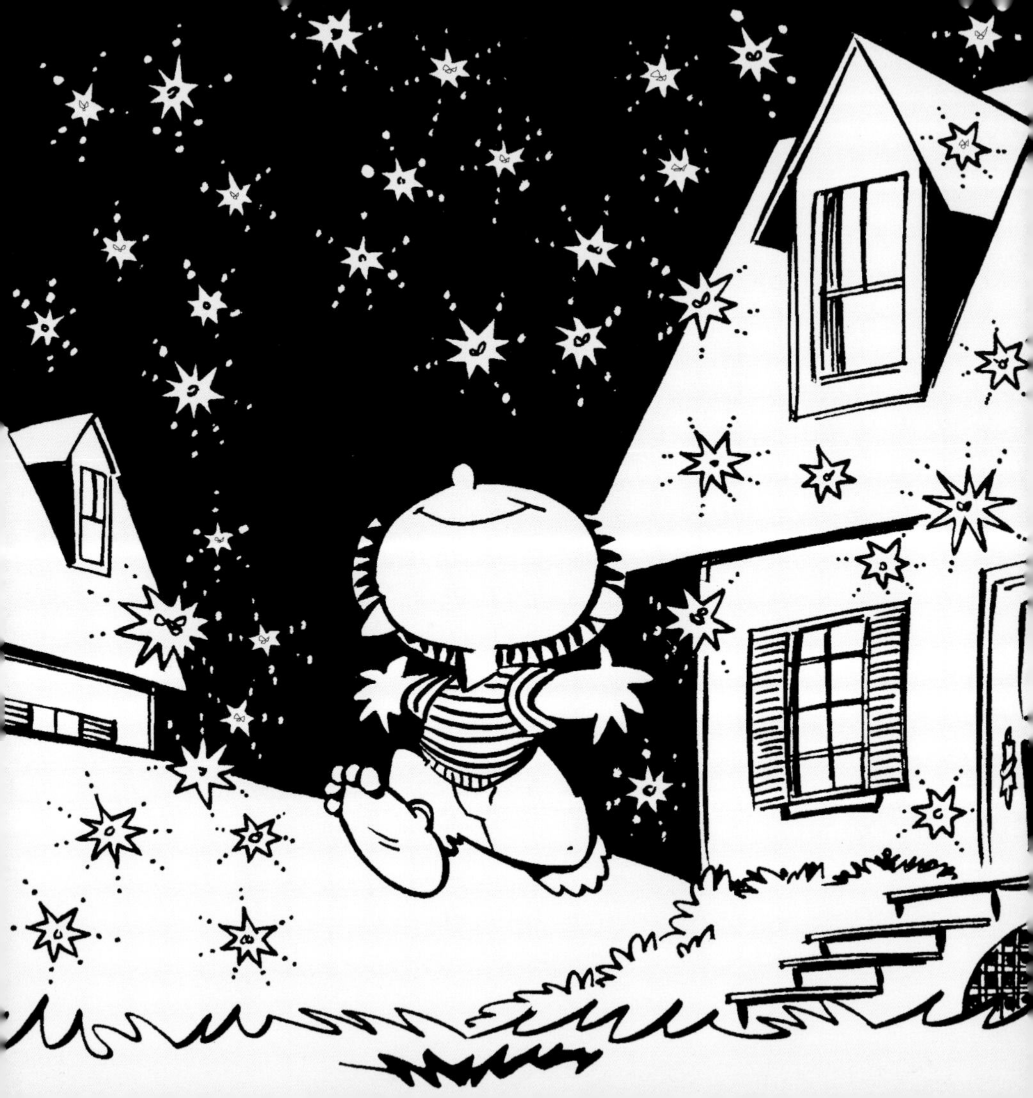

PEACE OF MIND
IS A BACKYARD
SPARKLING WITH
LIGHTNING BUGS

PEACE OF MIND IS HEARING THE VOICE YOU HOPED FOR

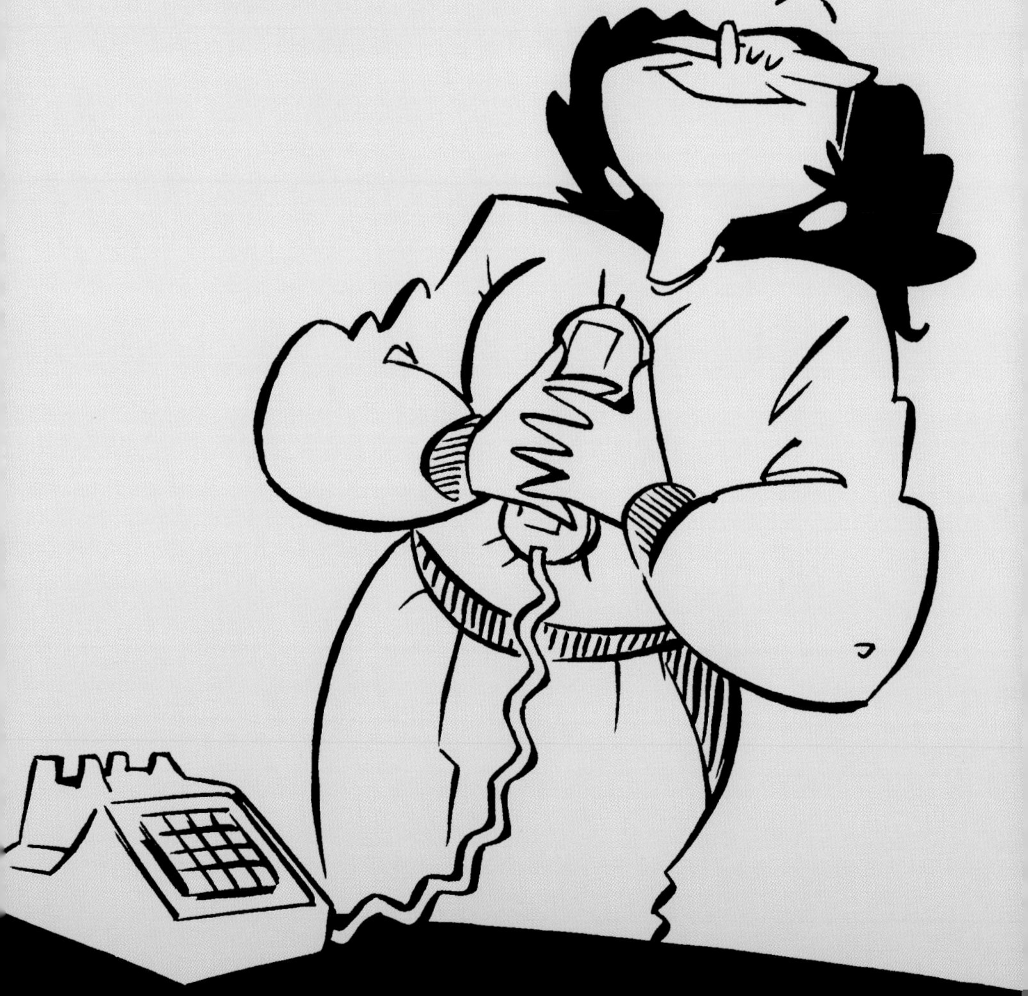

PEACE OF MIND IS HEARING THAT YOUR SCHOOL IS ON THE "SNOW DAY" LIST

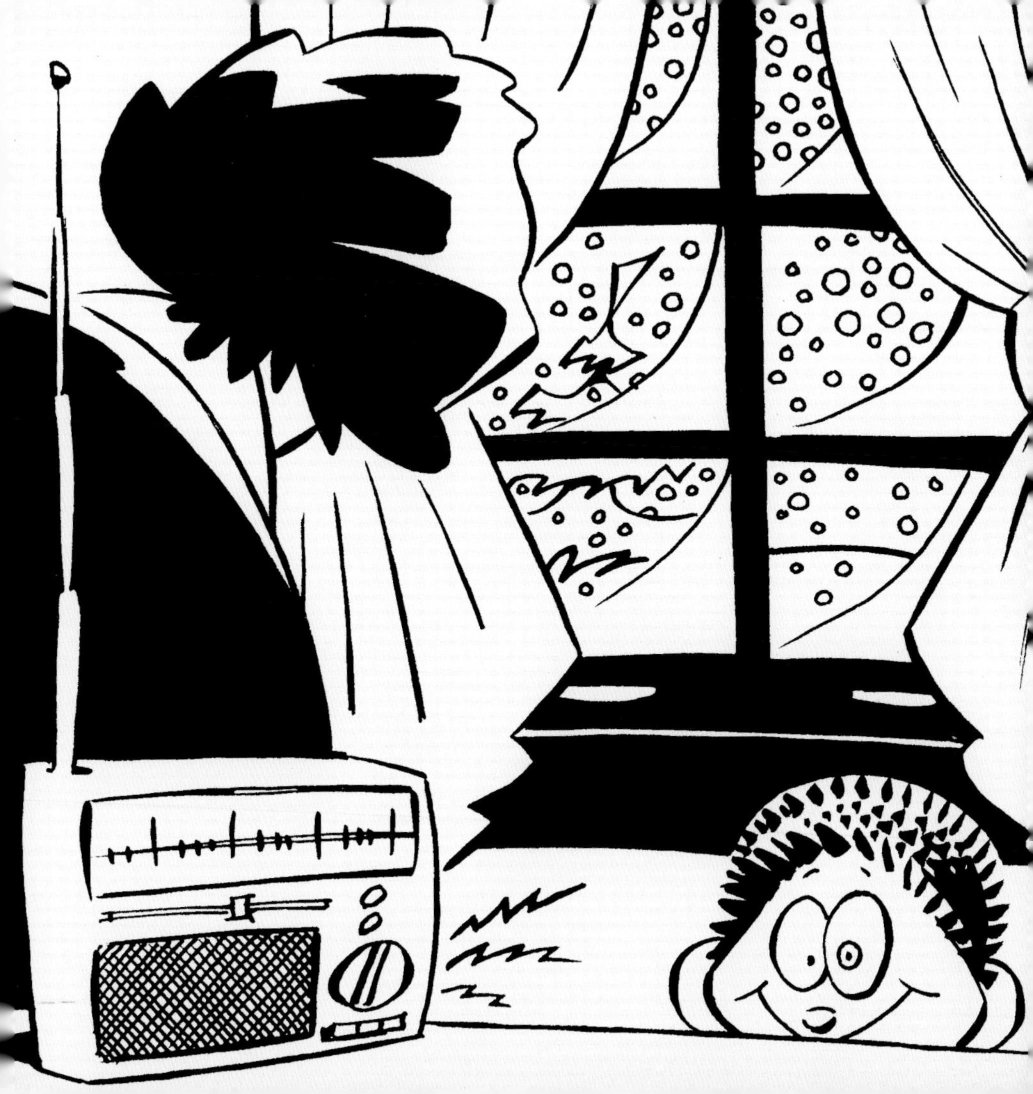

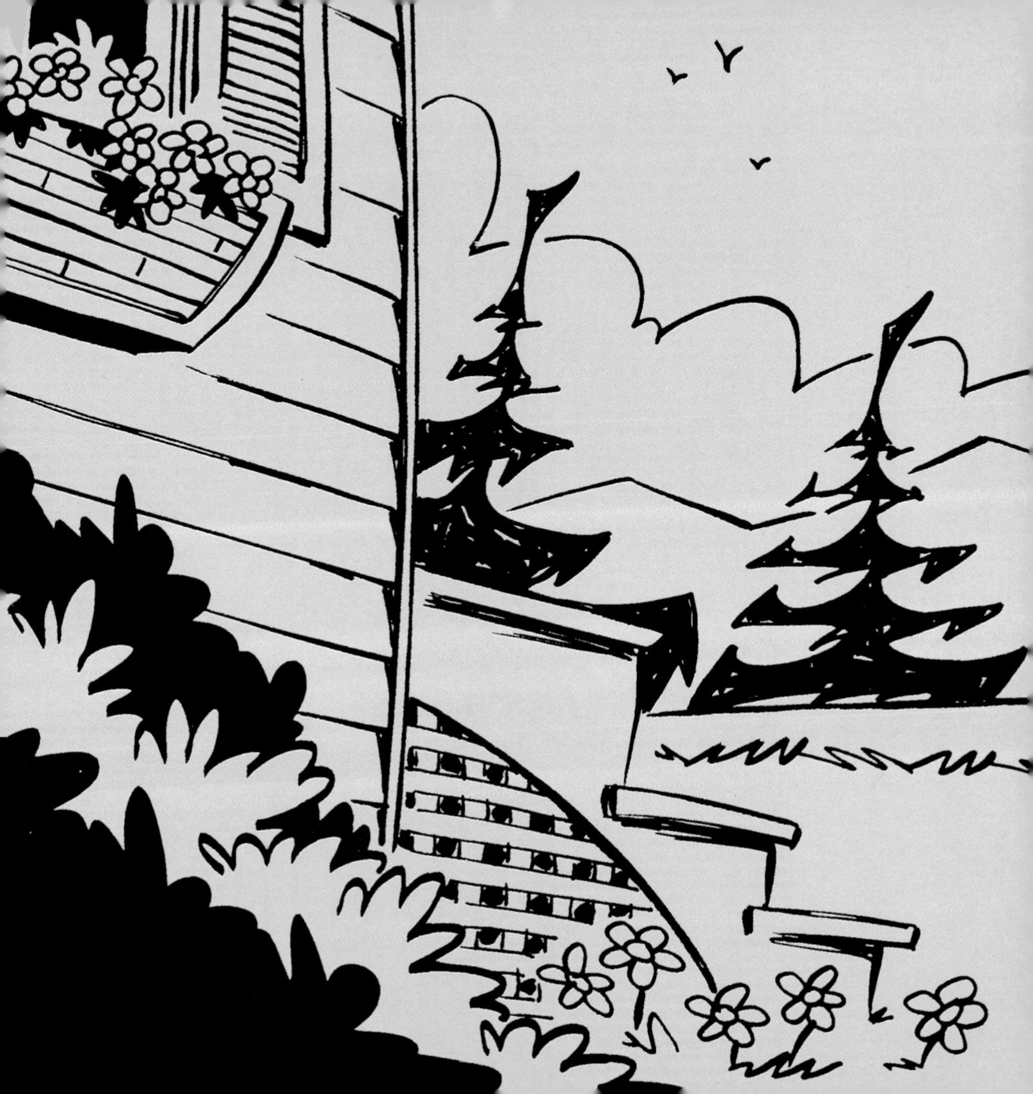

PEACE OF MIND IS FINDING YOUR HOUSE RIGHT WHERE YOU LEFT IT

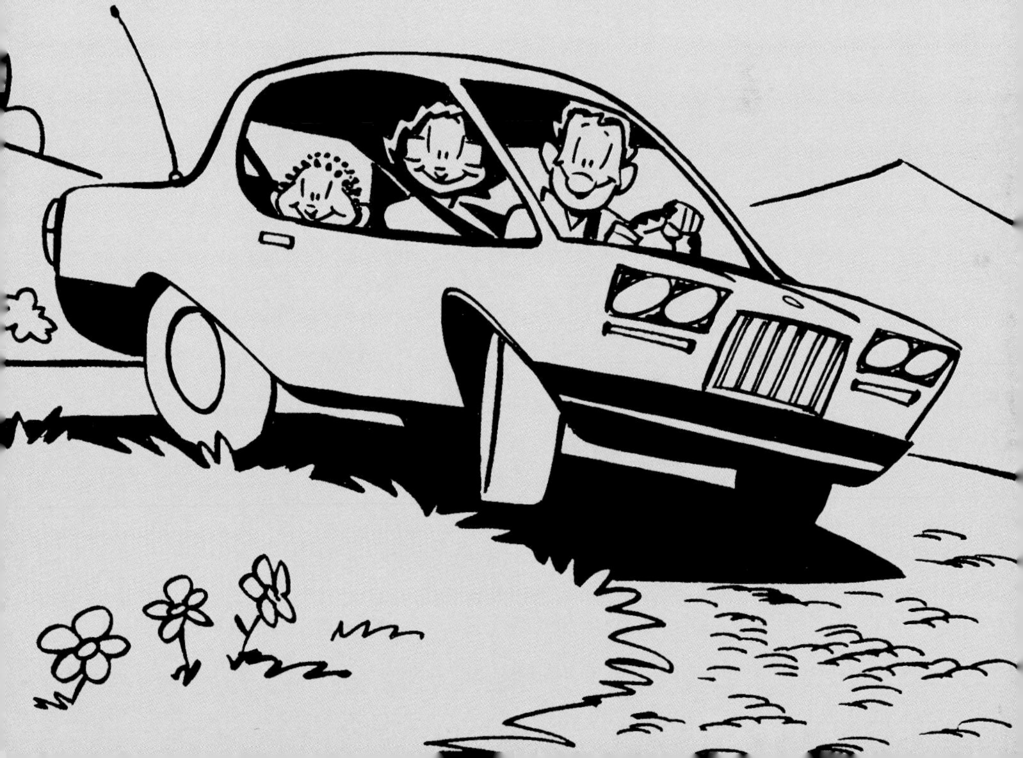

PEACE OF MIND IS KNOWING YOUR GUARDIAN ANGEL IS THERE

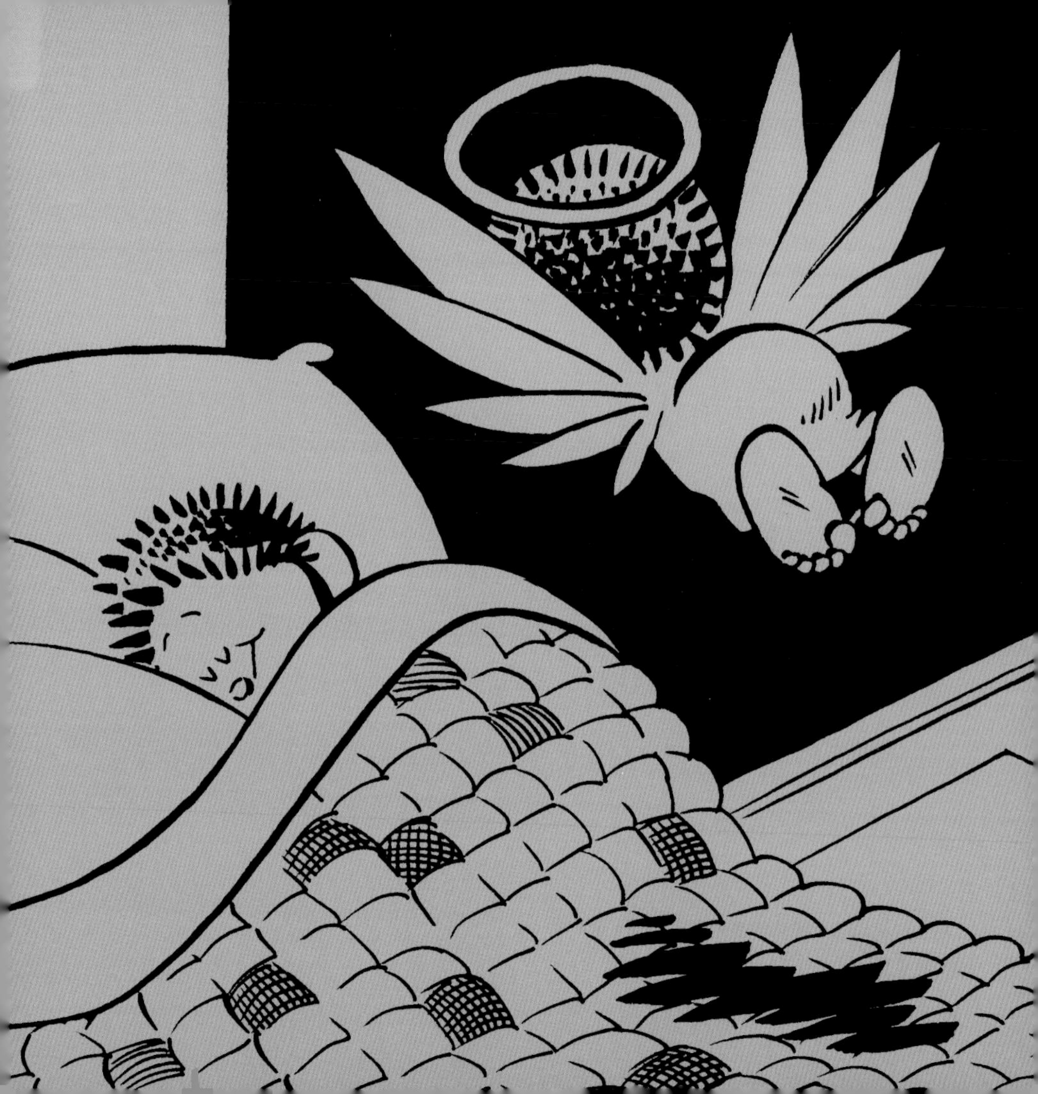

PEACE OF MIND
IS THE
COMBINED AROMAS
OF EGGS, BACON,
TOOTHPASTE,
ORANGES,
COFFEE, BREAD,
NEWSPAPERS
AND
AFTERSHAVE

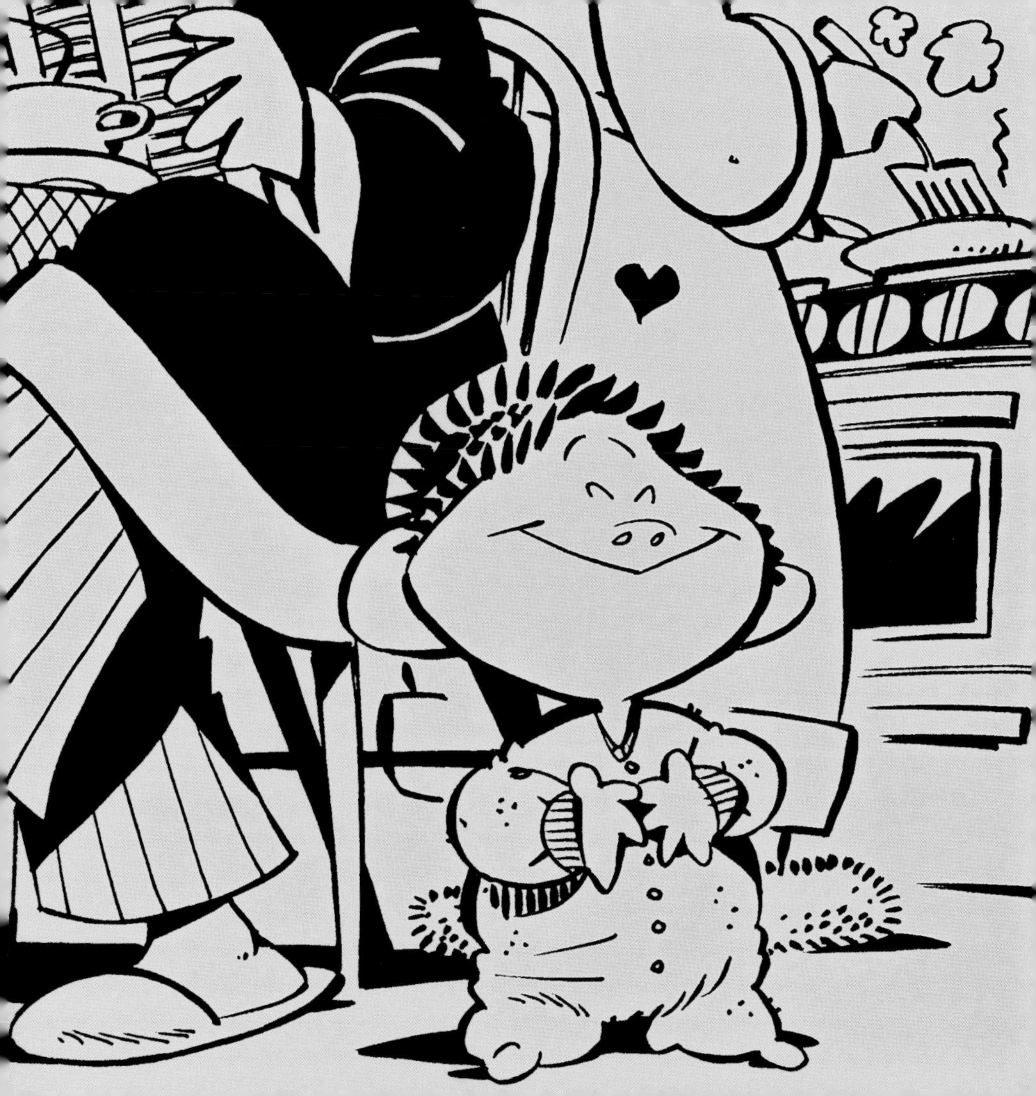

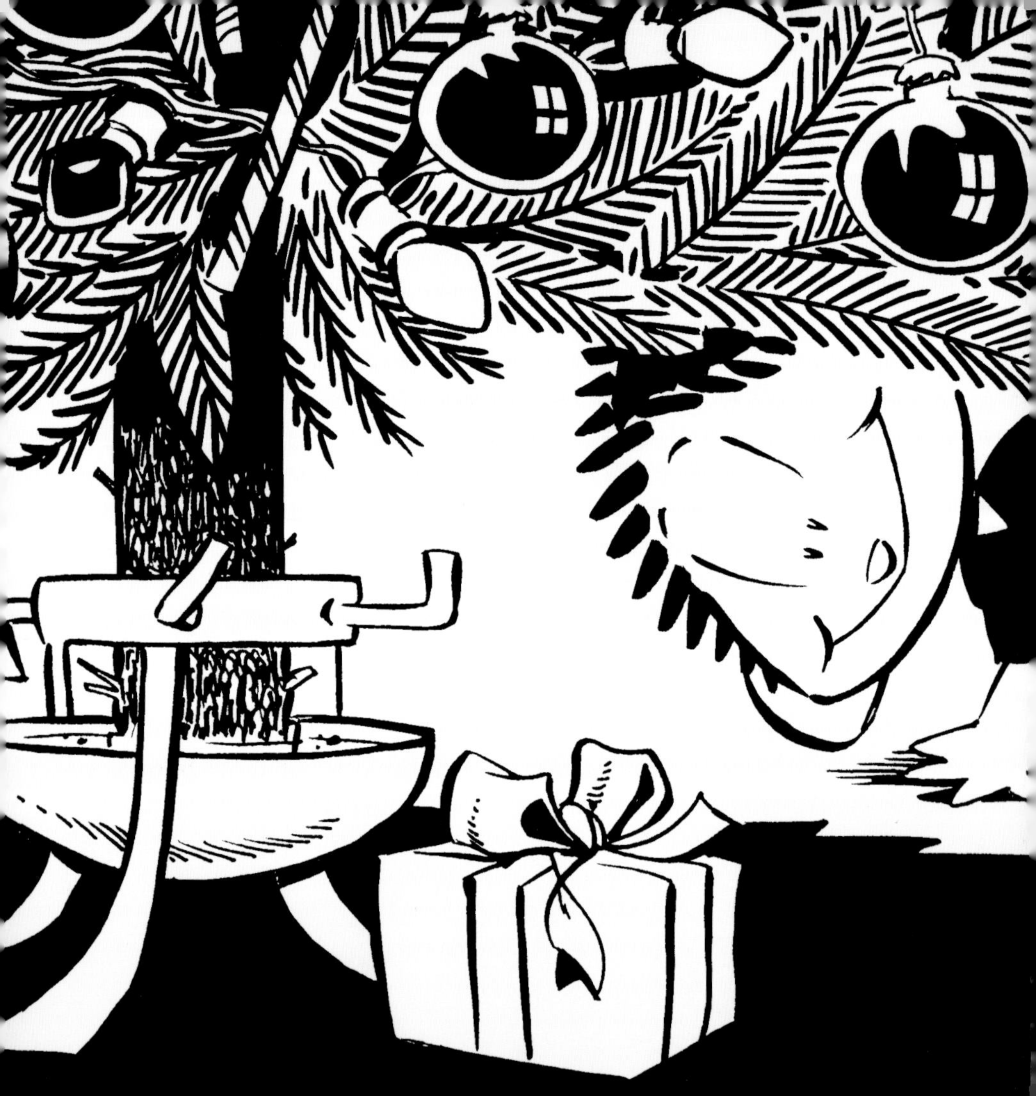

PEACE OF MIND
IS
FINDING
ONE MORE
PRESENT
UNDER
THE TREE

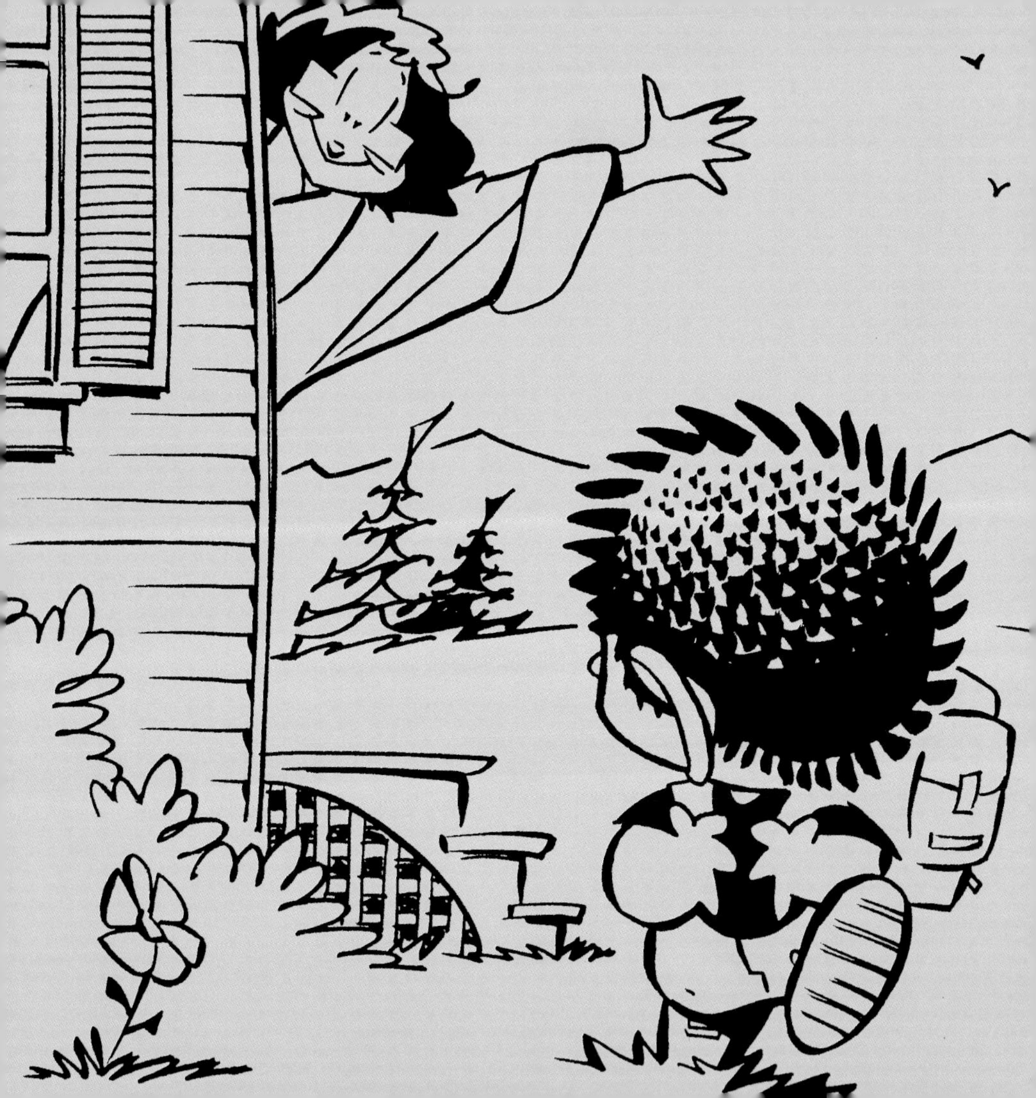

Peace of Mind is seeing your momma wave as you leave for school

PEACE OF MIND
IS KNOWING IF YOU
DON'T LIKE THE
SEASON,
THERE'S A NEW ONE
RIGHT AROUND
THE CORNER

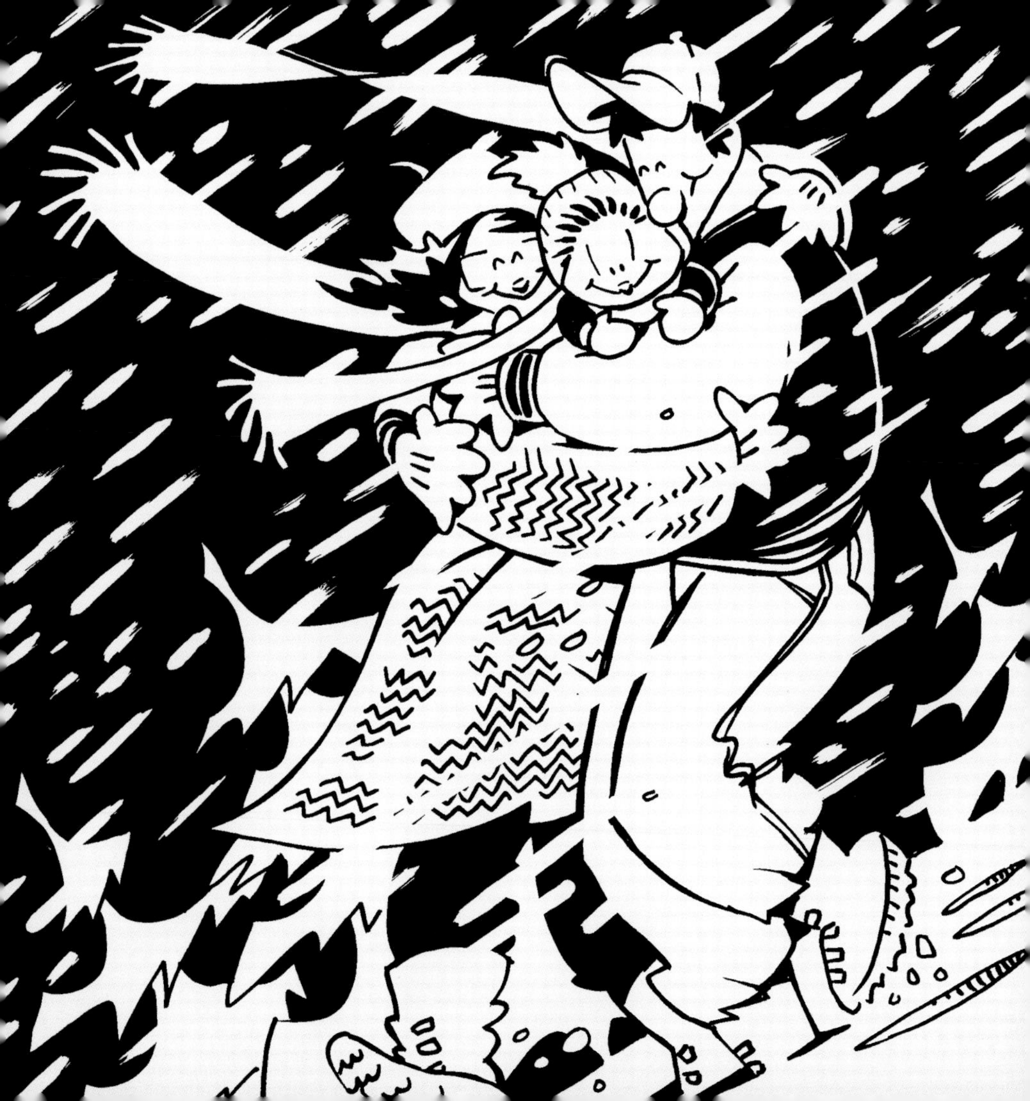

PEACE OF MIND IS FINDING A GREAT NEW PLACE FOR LUNCH

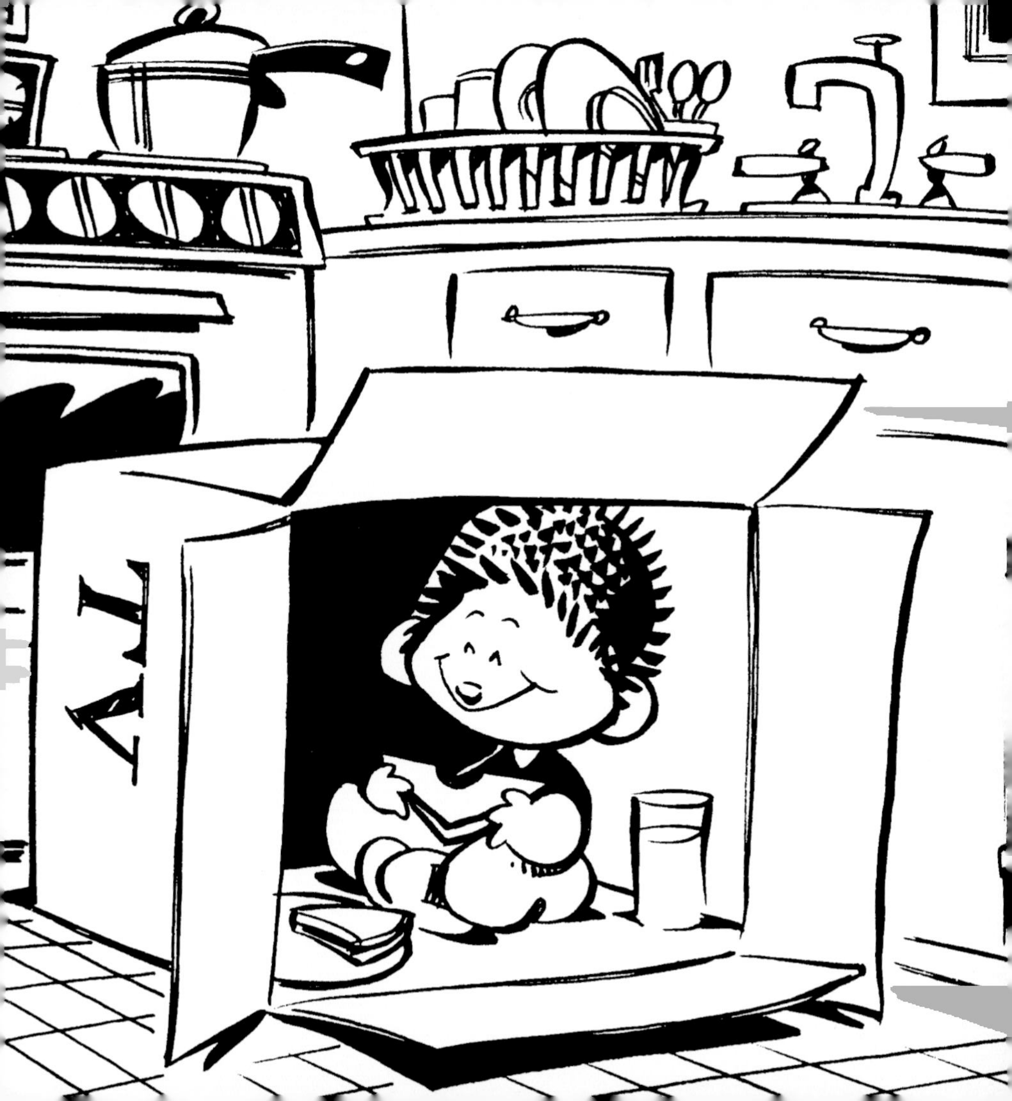
A.J

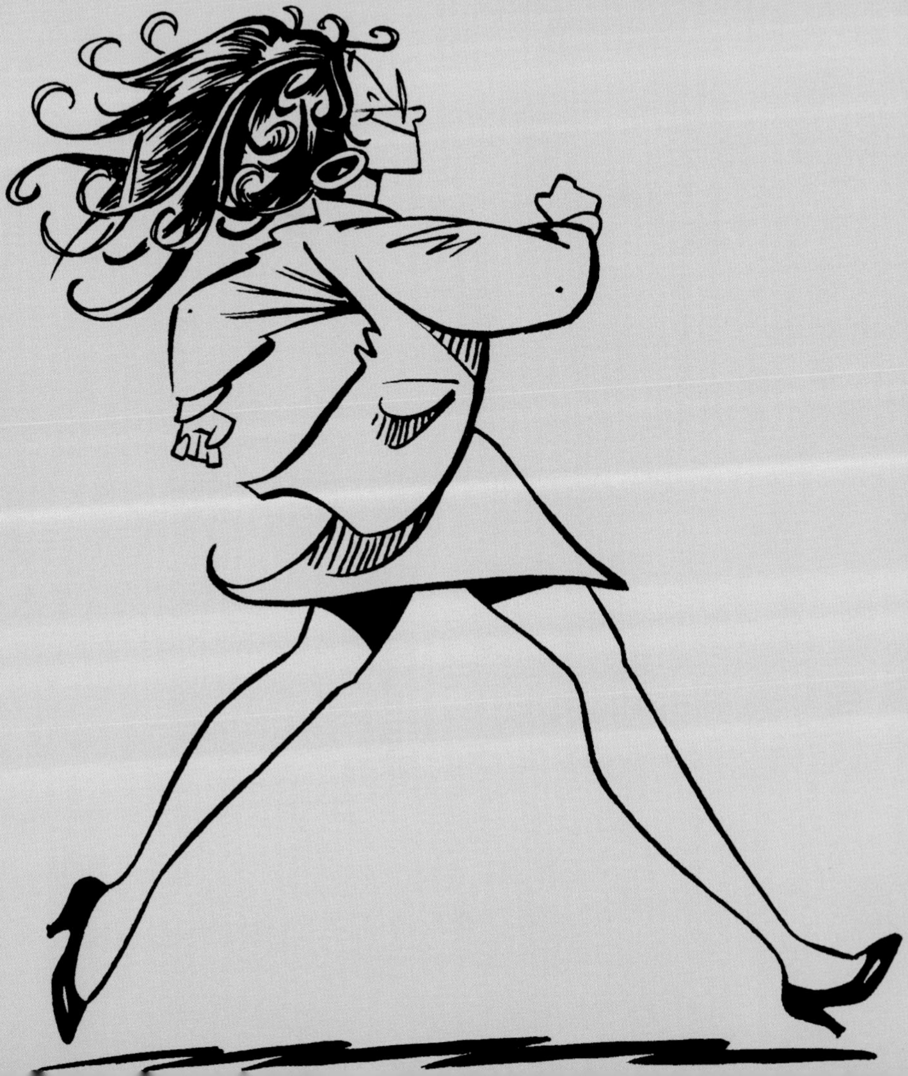

PEACE OF MIND IS KNOWING YOU'VE STILL GOT WHAT IT TAKES

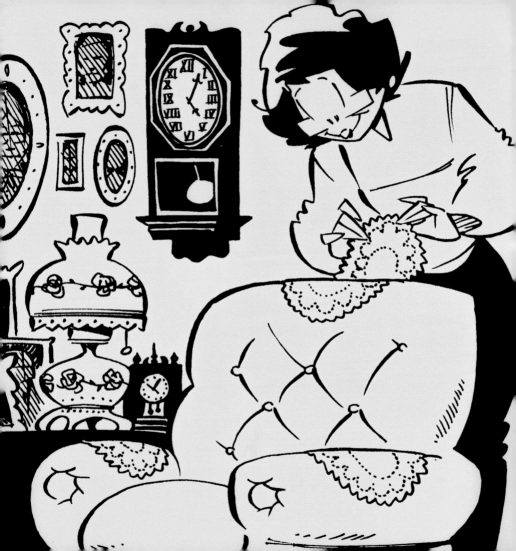

Peace of Mind
is
anything
old-fashioned

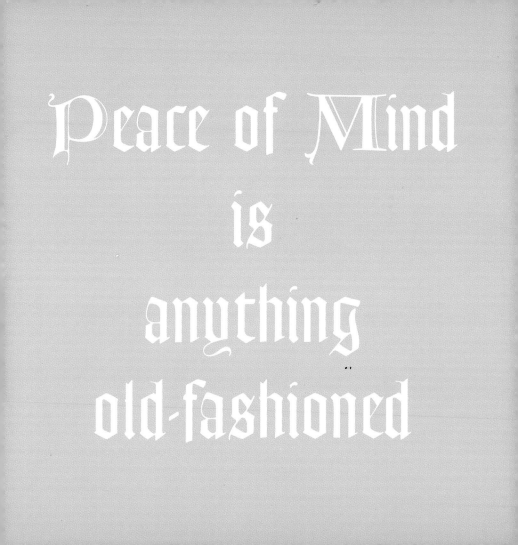

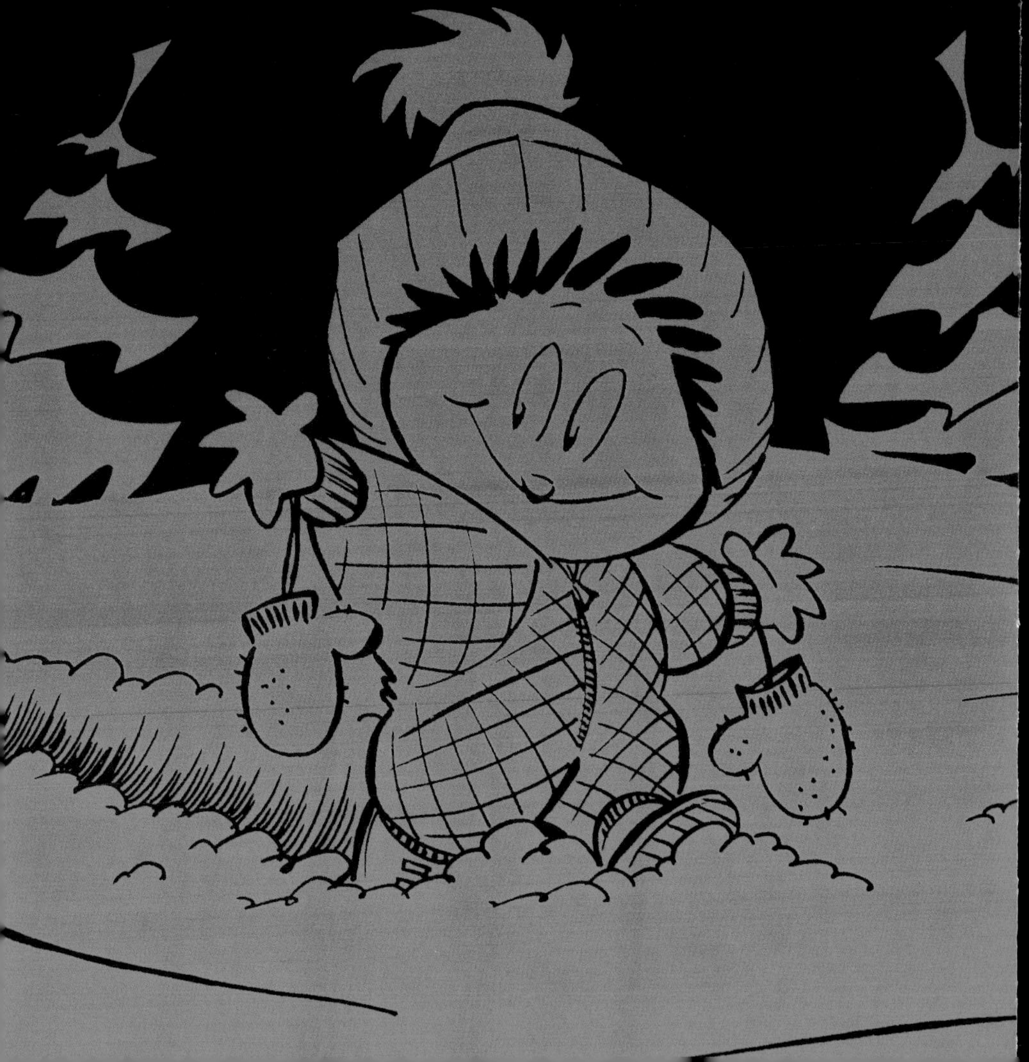

PEACE OF MIND IS A PROPERLY INSTALLED MITTEN STRING

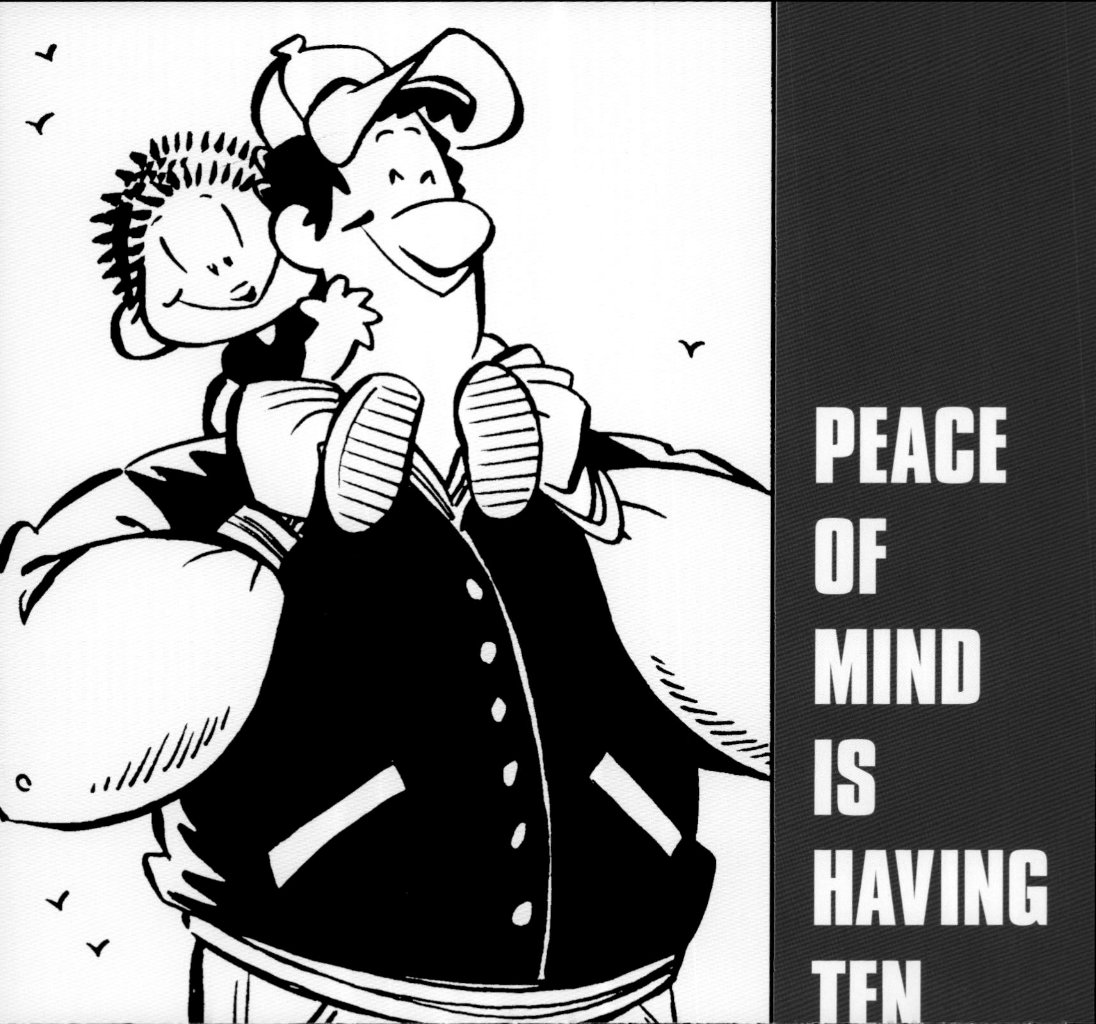

PEACE OF MIND IS HAVING TEN

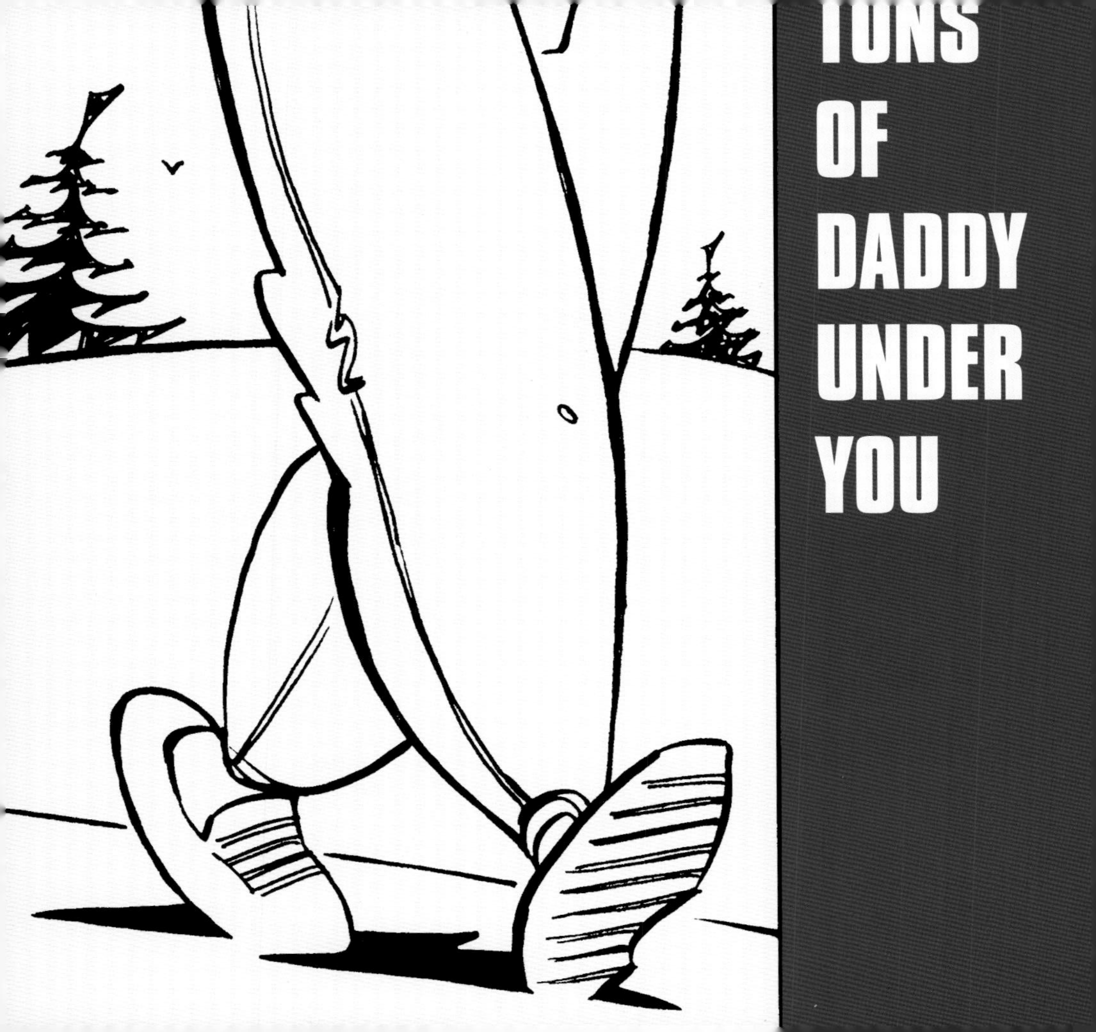

TONS
OF
DADDY
UNDER
YOU

PEACE OF MIND IS KNOWING A SHORTCUT

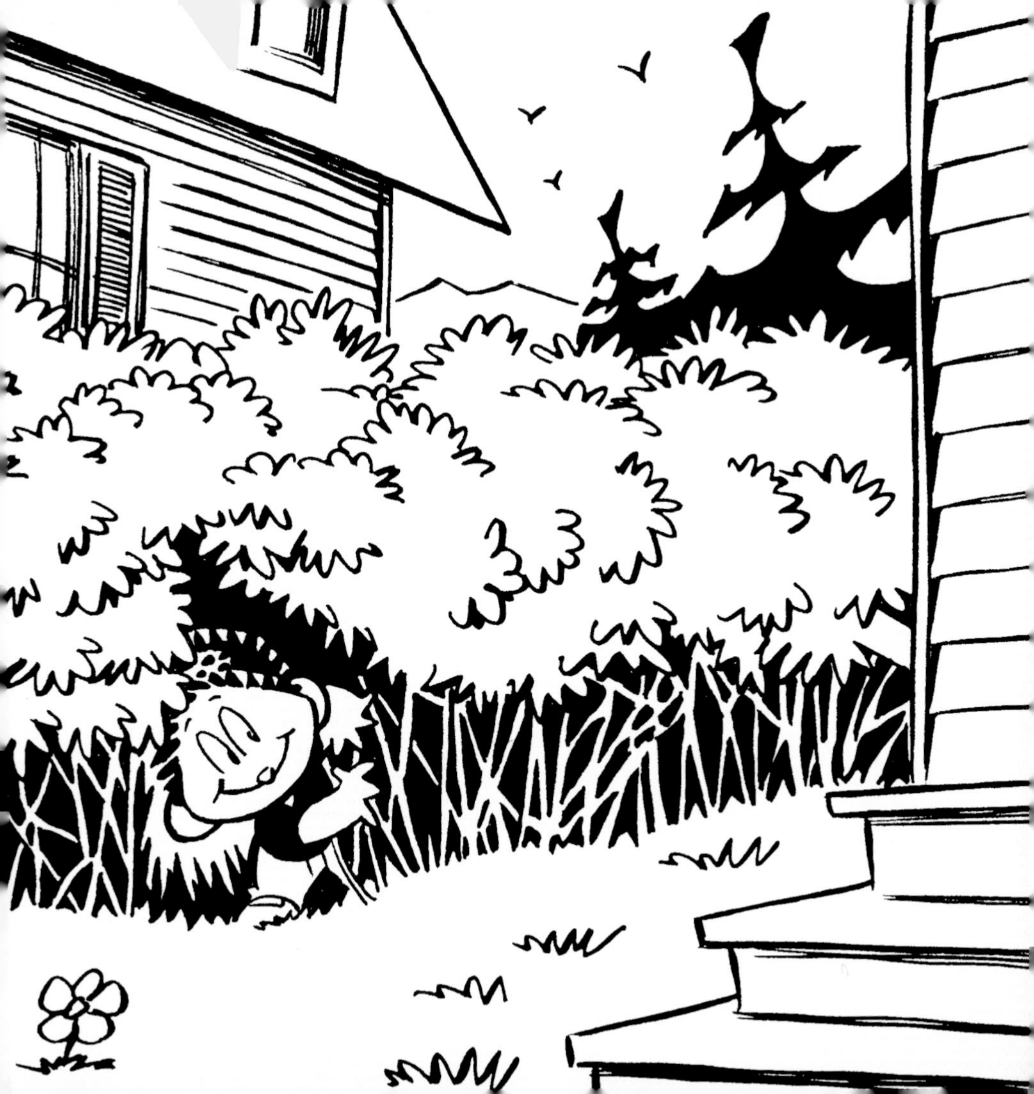

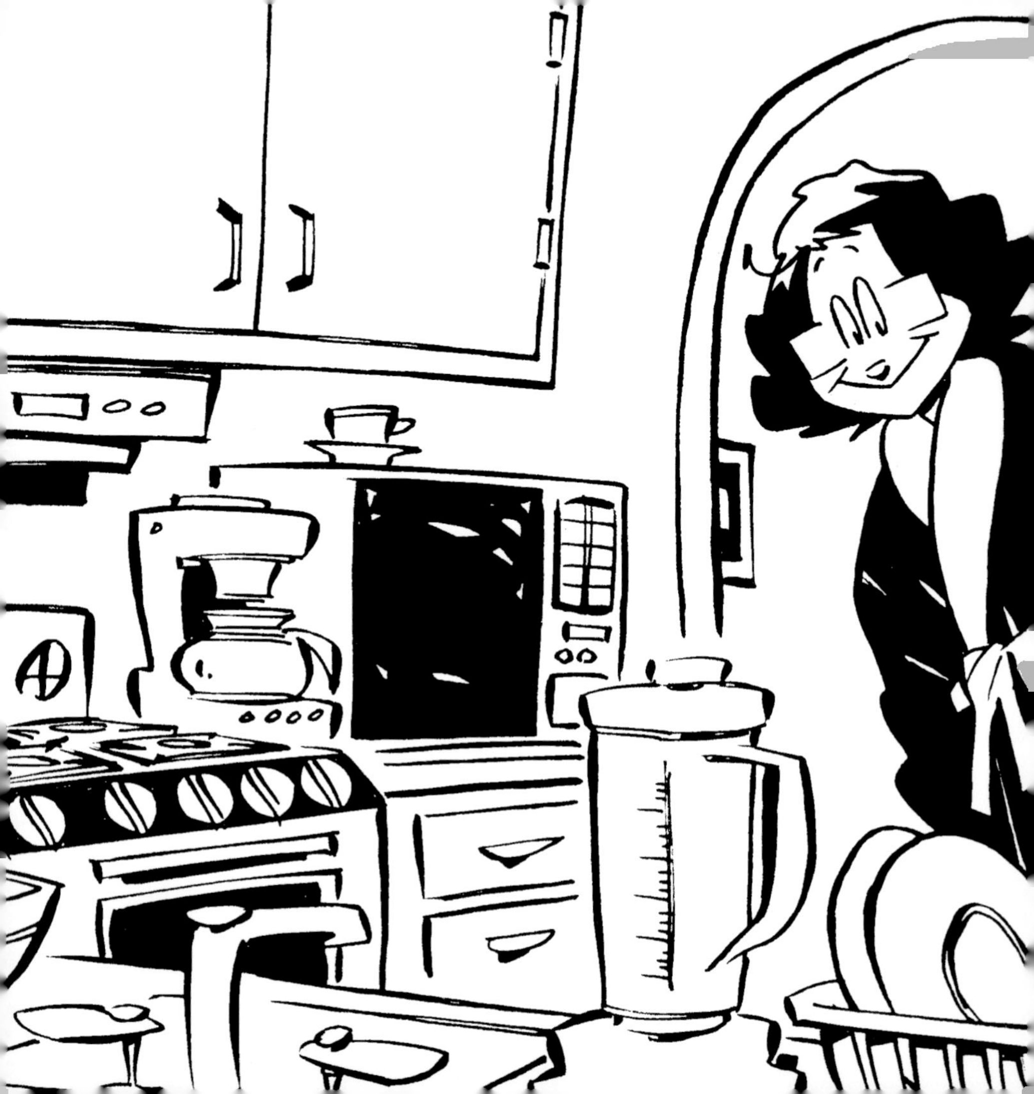

PEACE OF MIND
IS FINDING
EVERYTHING
JUST THE WAY
YOU LEFT IT
THE NIGHT
BEFORE

PEACE OF MIND
IS
NOT HAVING TO
ASK
DIRECTIONS

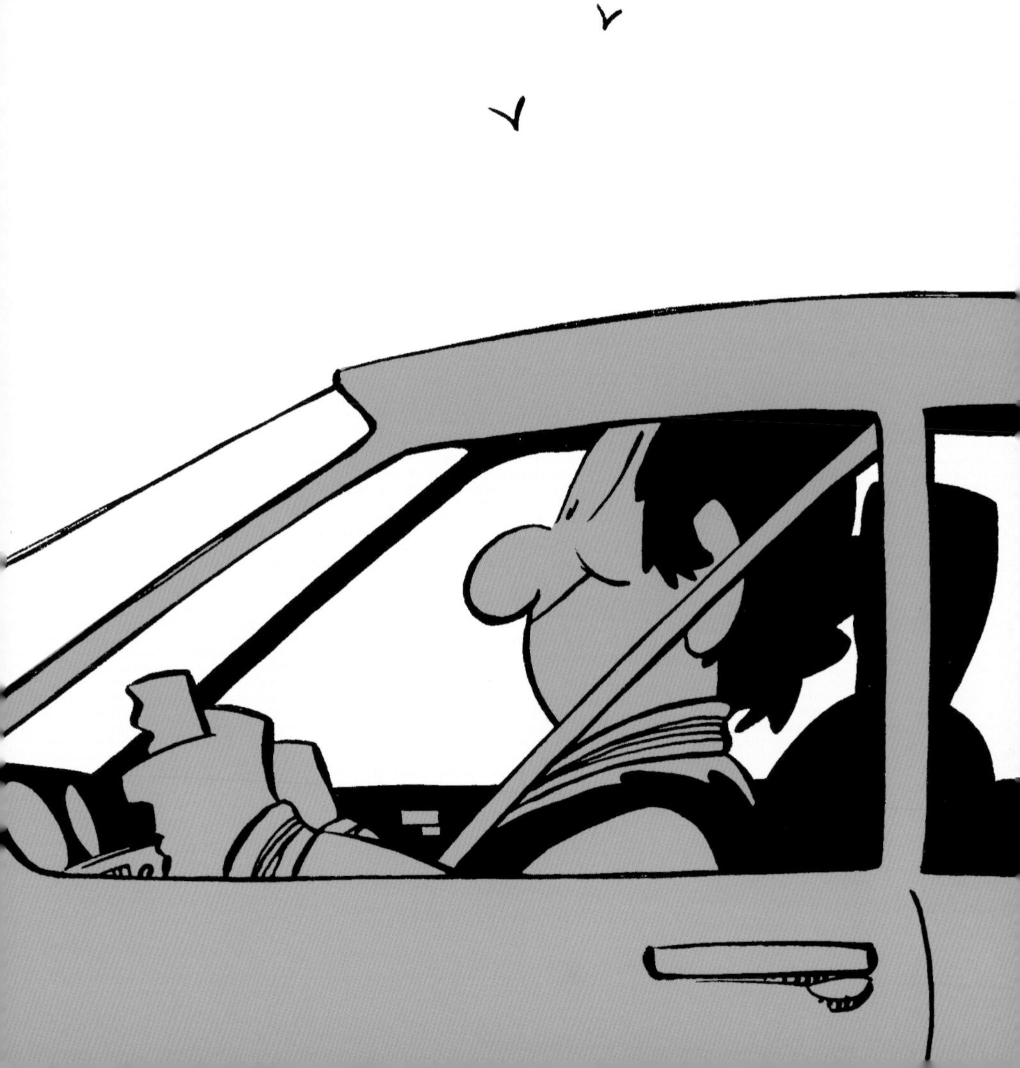

PEACE OF MIND
IS
ONE CAPFUL OF
BUBBLE BATH
STASHED AWAY
FOR
EMERGENCIES

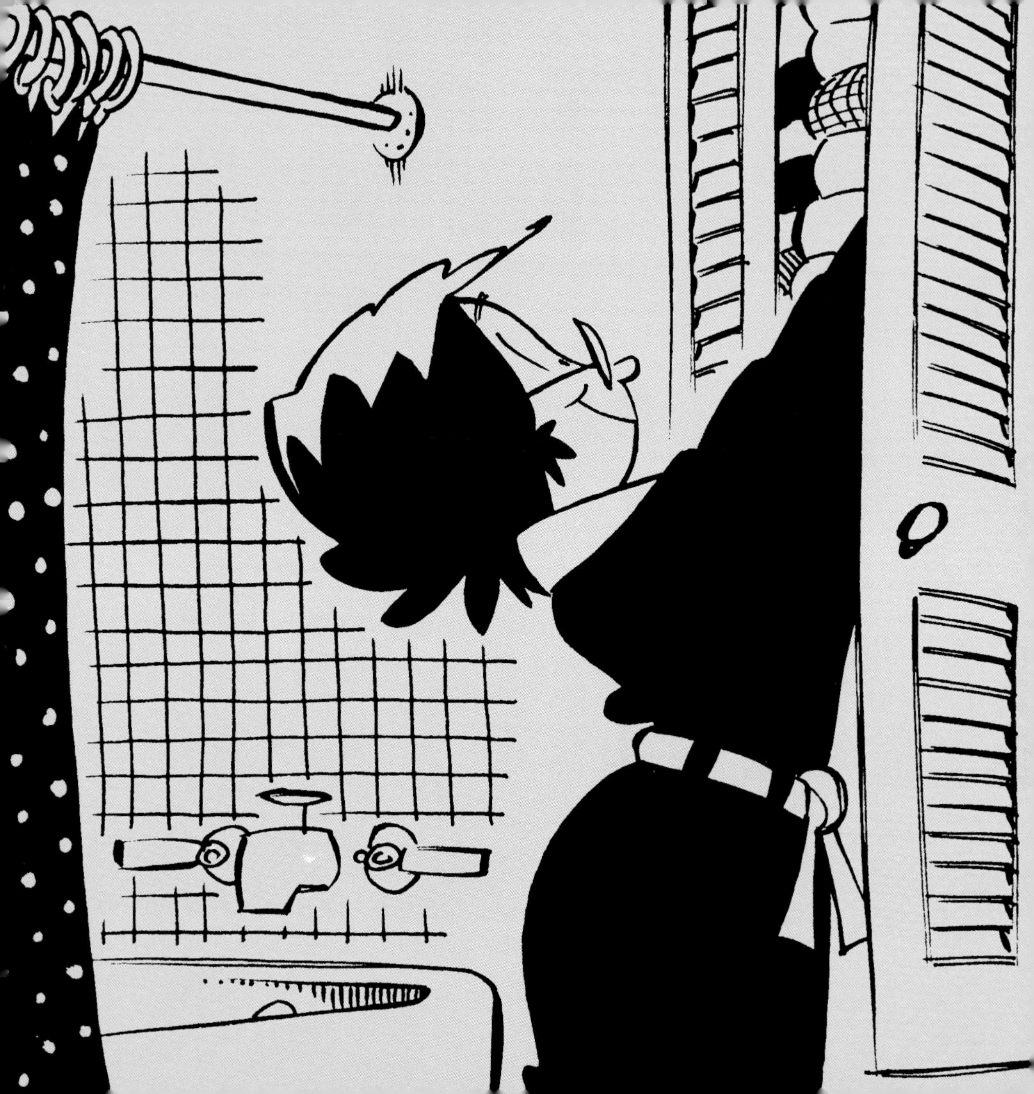

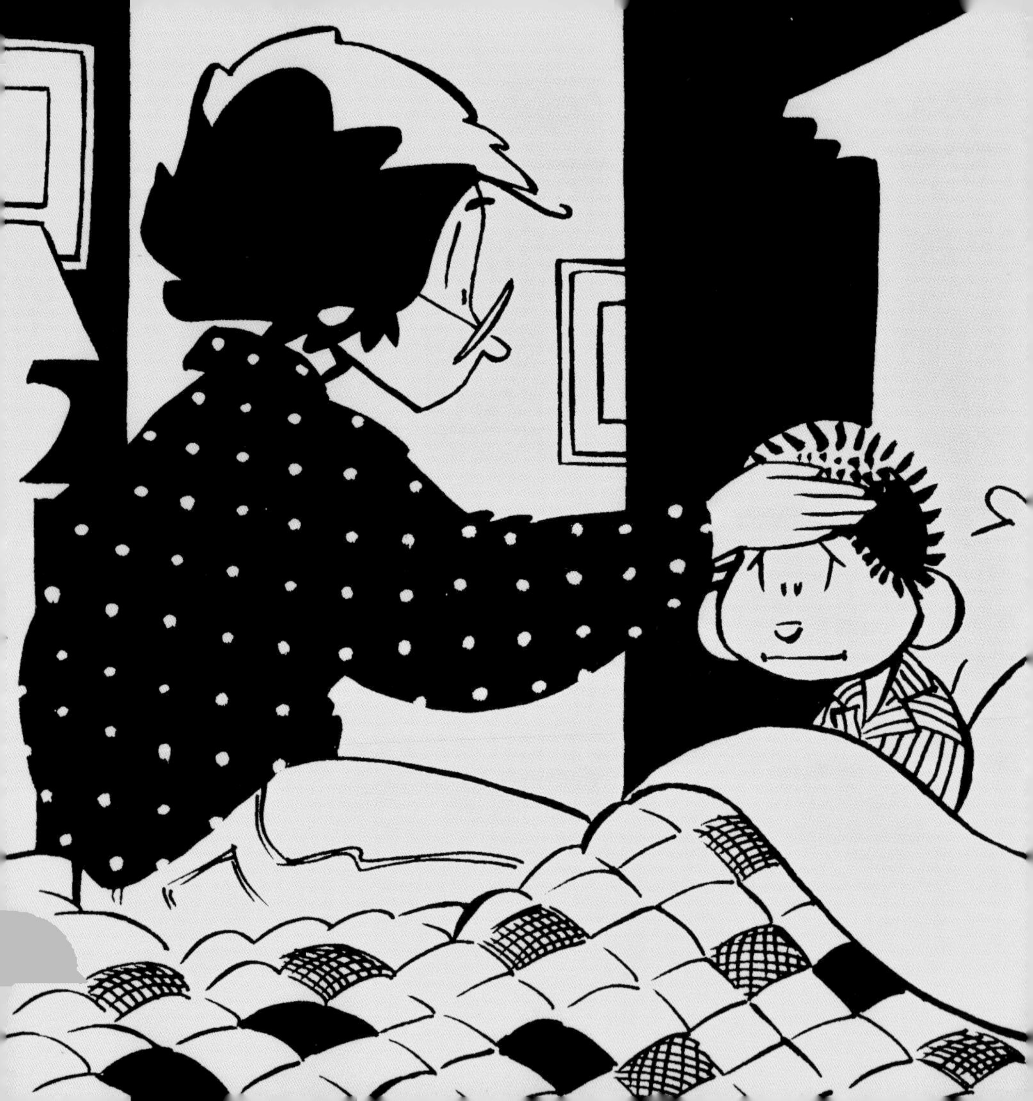

PEACE OF MIND
IS SOMEONE
TO FEEL YOUR
FOREHEAD

PEACE OF MIND IS KNOWING SOMEONE SAVED YOU A SEAT

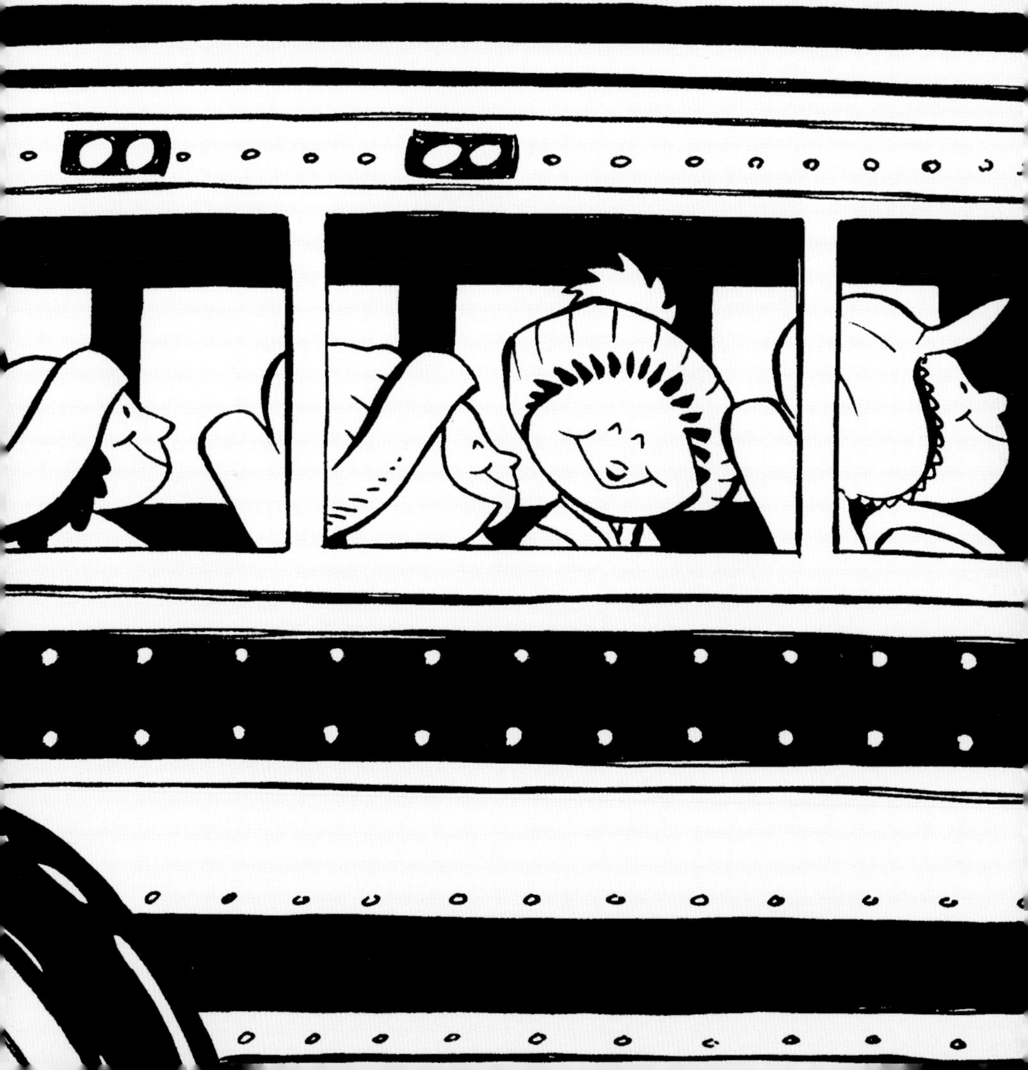

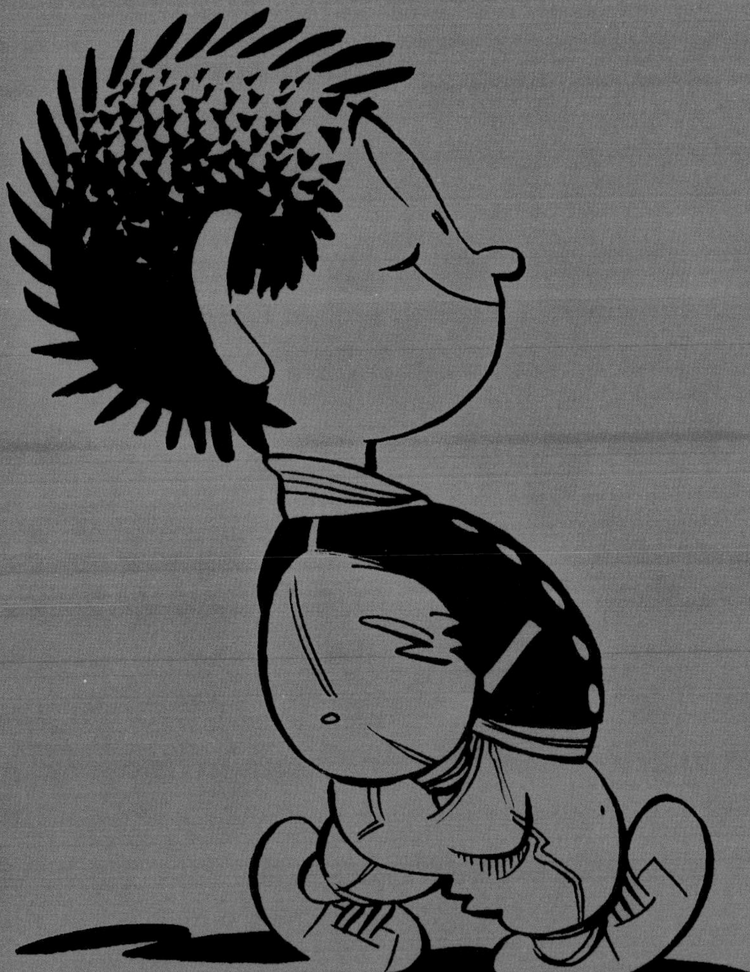

PEACE ON MIND IS HAVING YOUR GRANDFATHER'S LUCKY SILVER DOLLAR IN YOUR POCKET

PEACE OF MIND IS HAVING ALL YOUR COUPONS READY

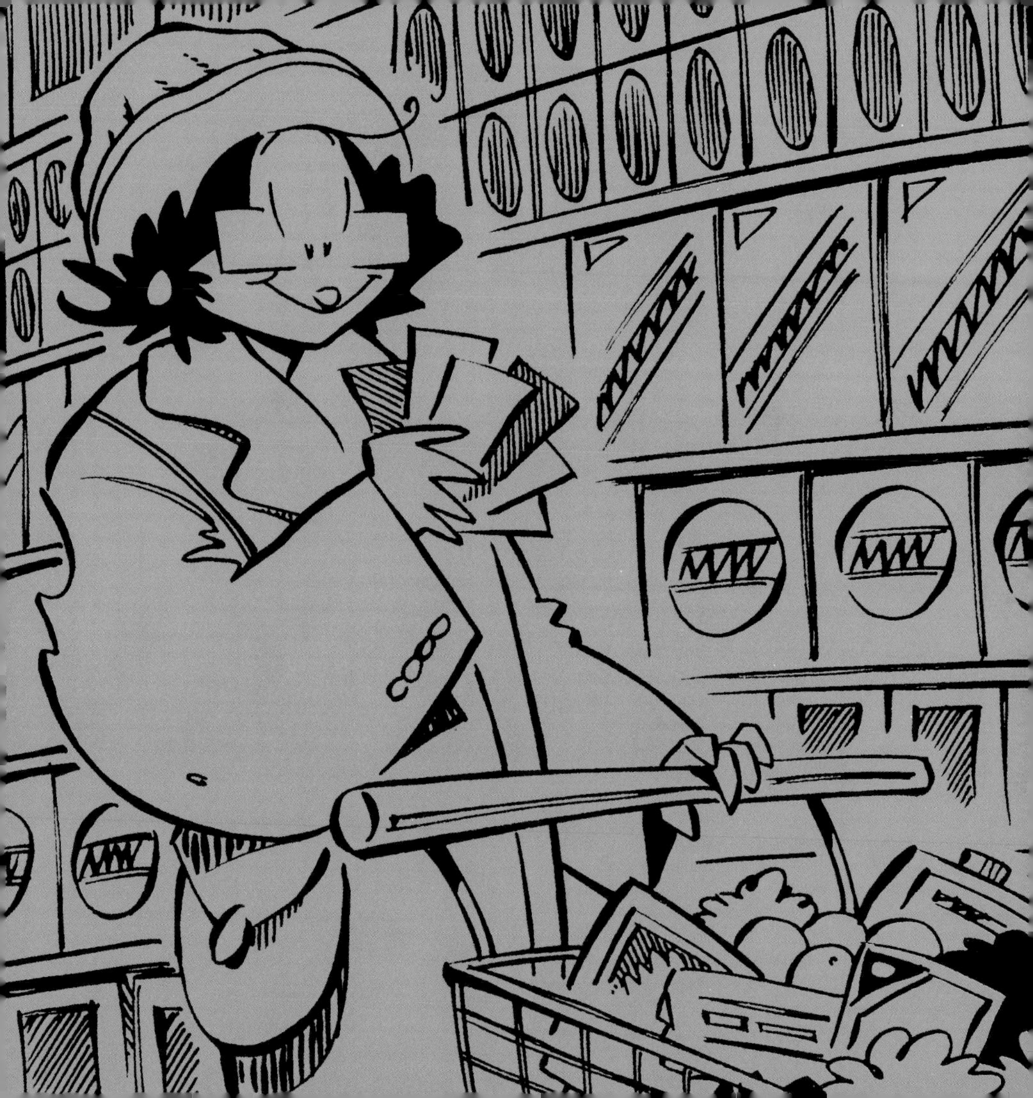

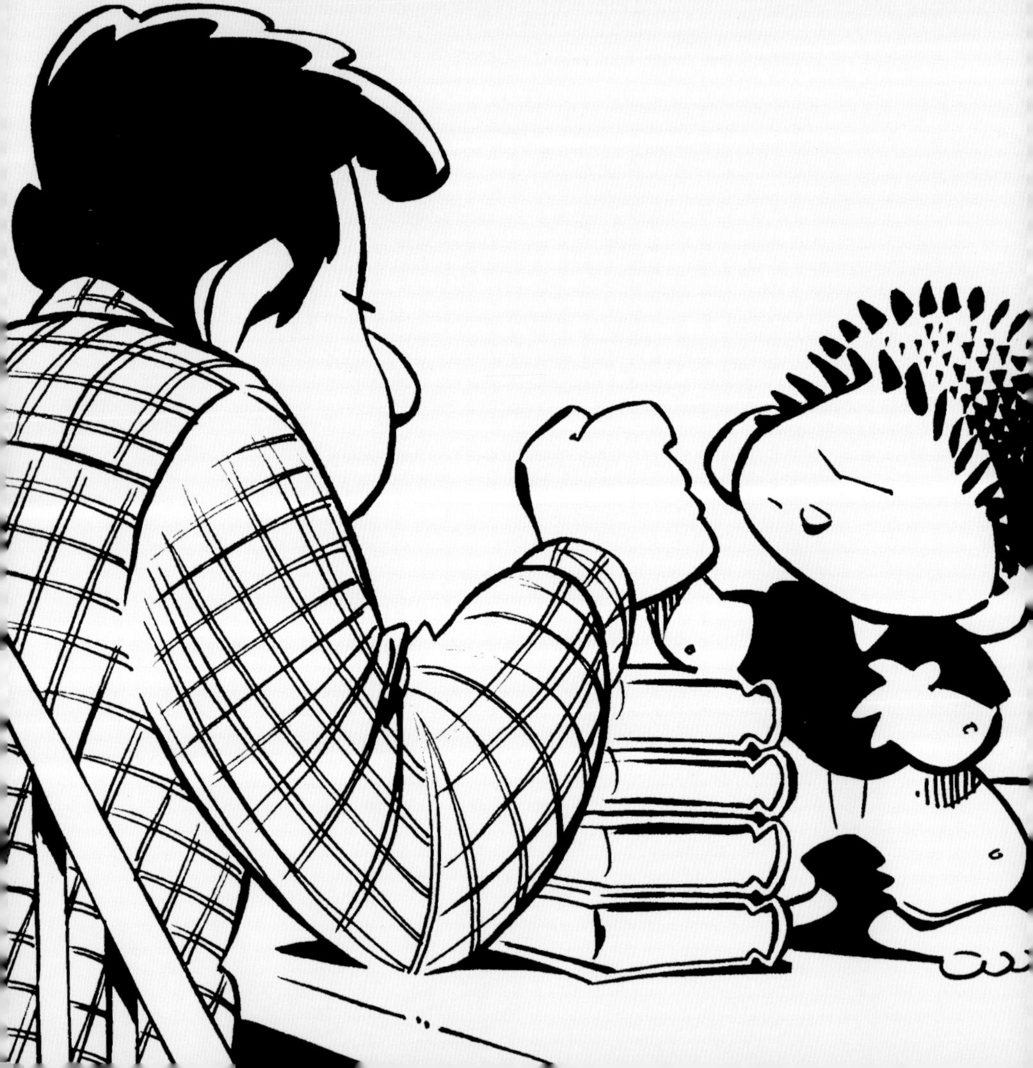

PEACE OF MIND
IS FOUR BOOKS
UNDER YOUR ELBOW
TO MAKE THE
ARM WRESTLING MATCH
FAIR

PEACE OF MIND IS A LITTLE PAT ON THE BACK NOW AND THEN

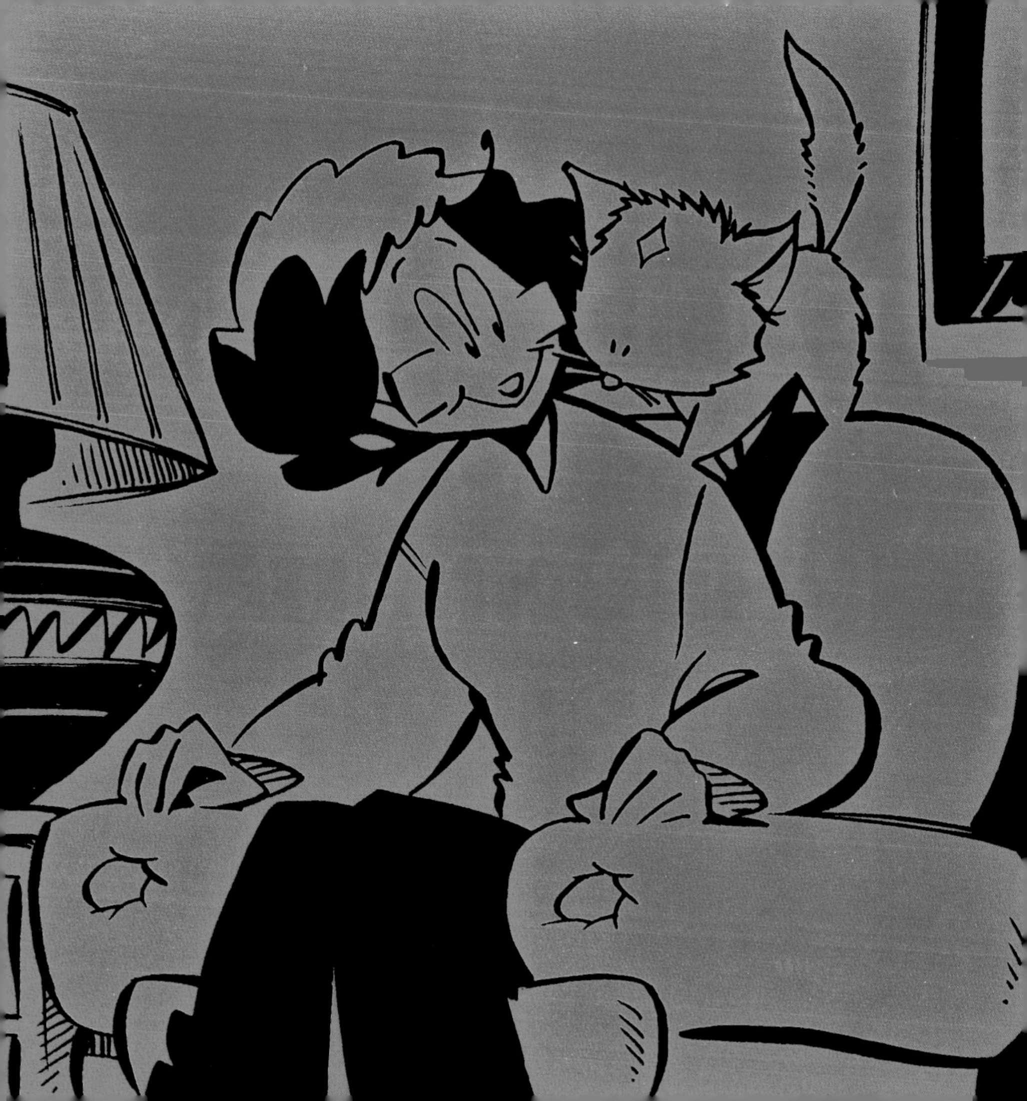

PEACE OF MIND IS PEPPERMINT BREATH

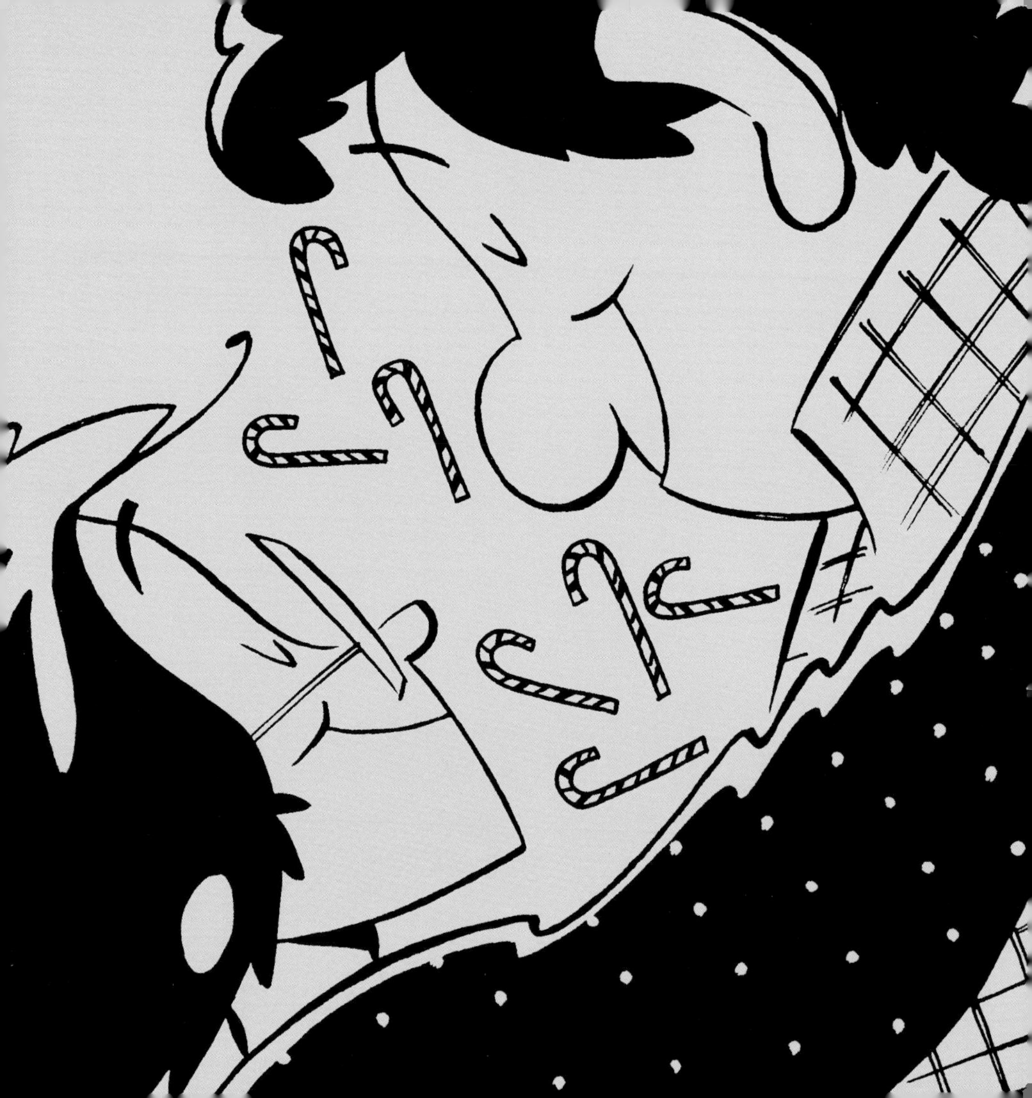

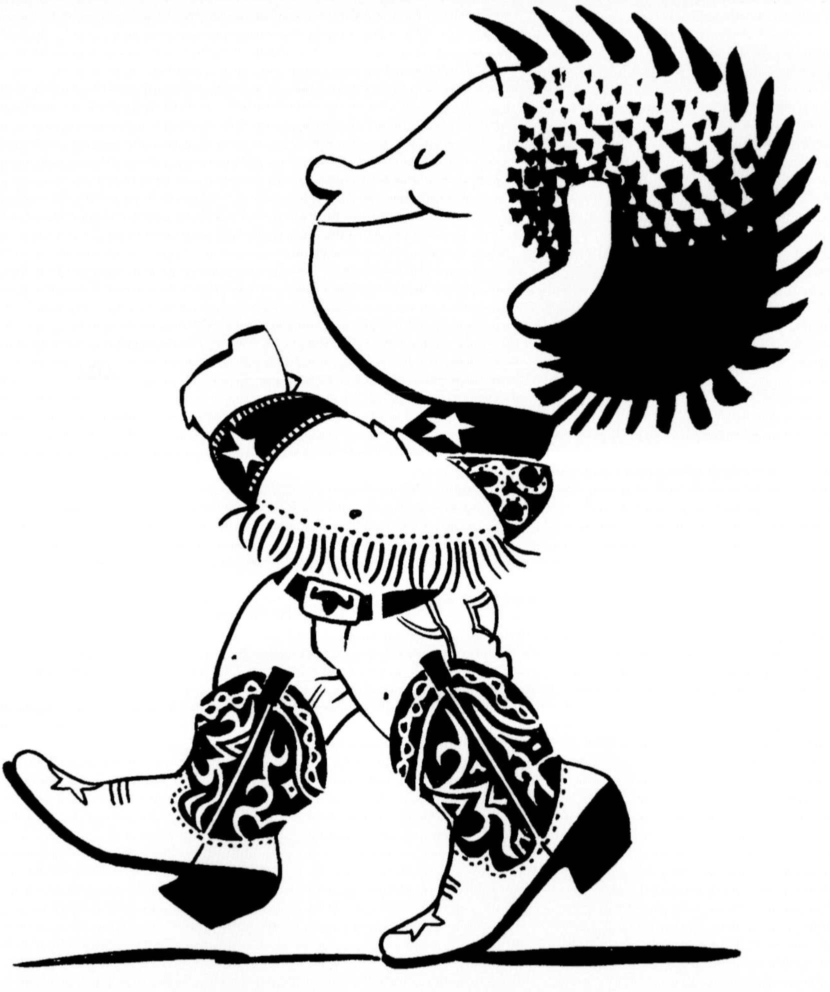

PEACE OF MIND
IS
OWNING
MANLY
FOOTWEAR

Peace of Mind
is deciding to
let things be

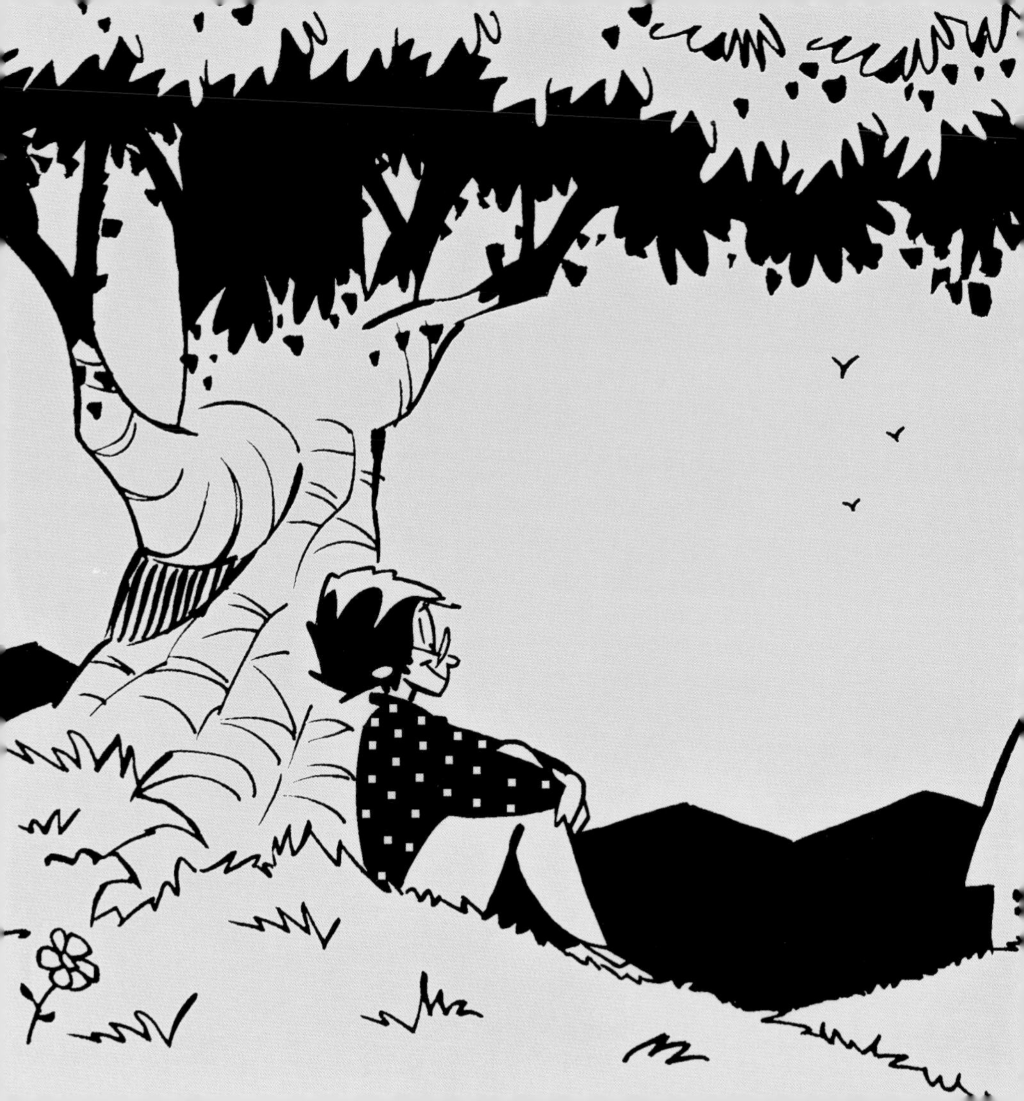

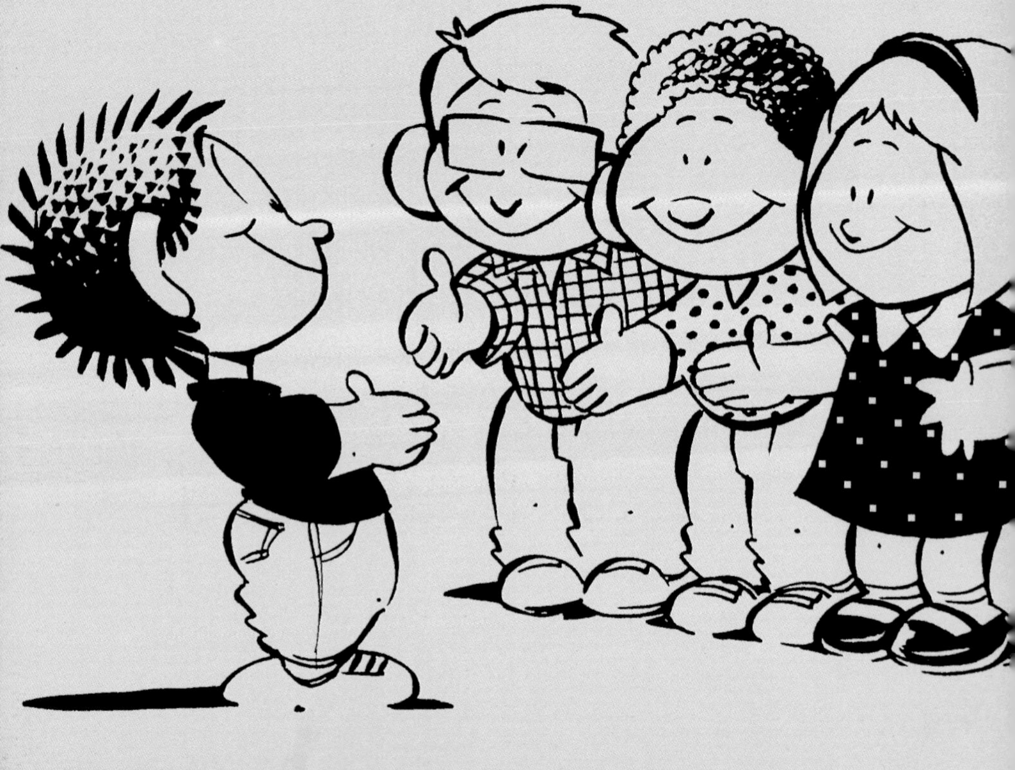

PEACE OF MIND IS FRIENDLY FACES WHEN YOU'RE THE NEW KID

PEACE OF MIND IS AN OCCASIONAL REPEAL OF THE NO-MUDDY-HANDS LAW

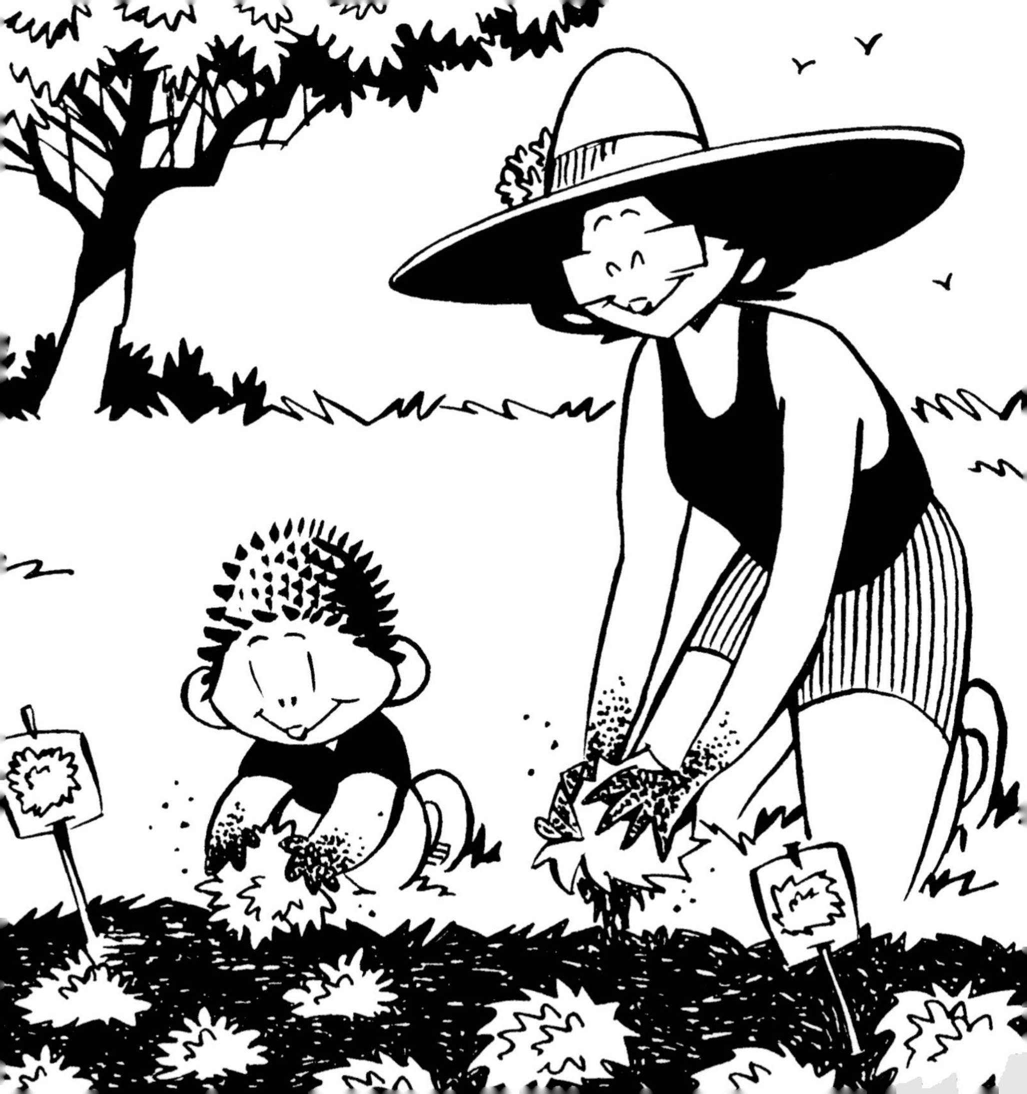

AN
UNHURRIED
BELLY RUB
IS
PEACE OF MIND
FOR THE
GIVER
AND THE
GETTER

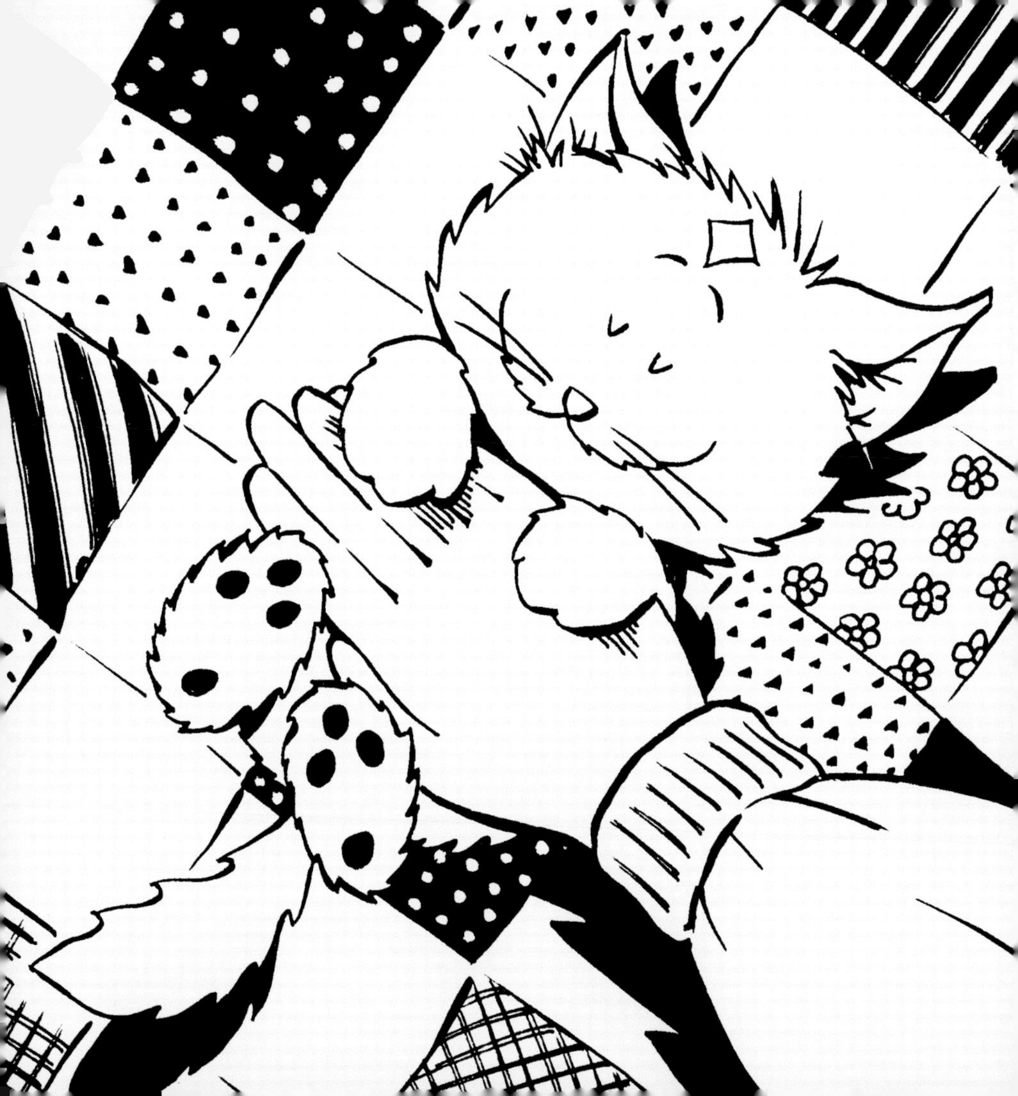

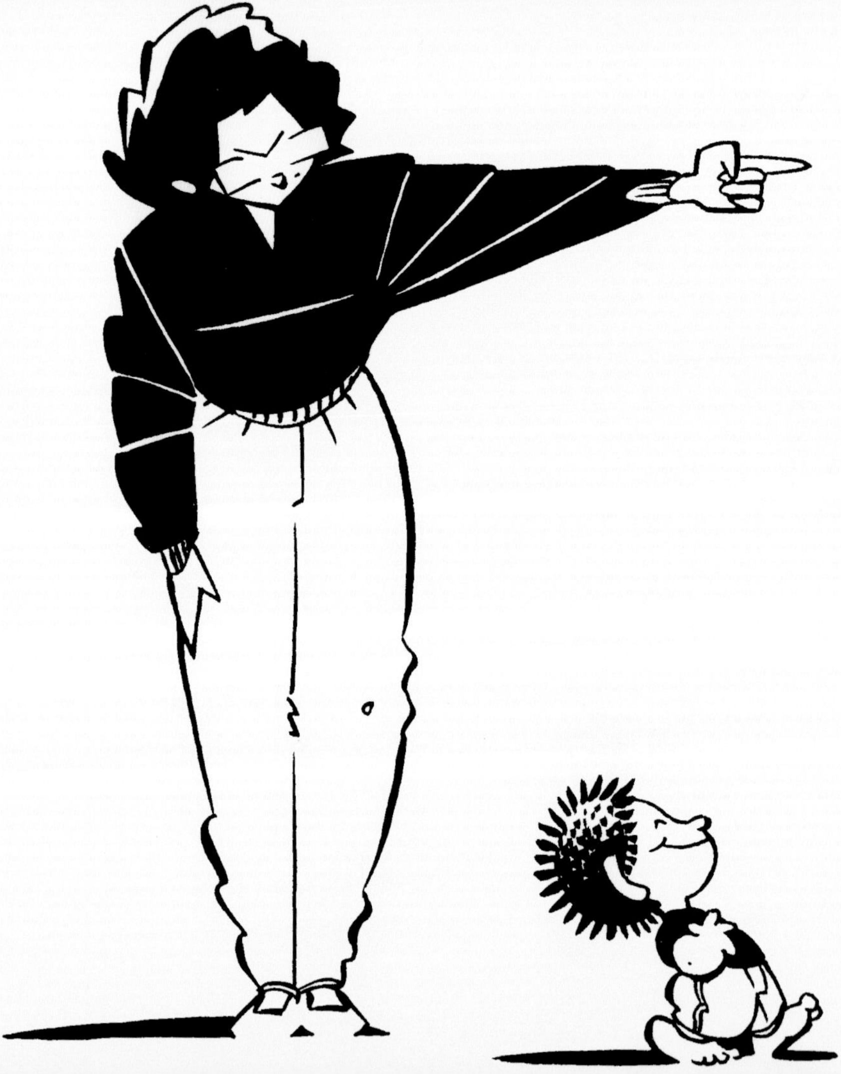

PEACE OF MIND IS KNOWING WHO'S IN CHARGE

PEACE OF MIND IS A LADYBUG DROPPING BY FOR A VISIT

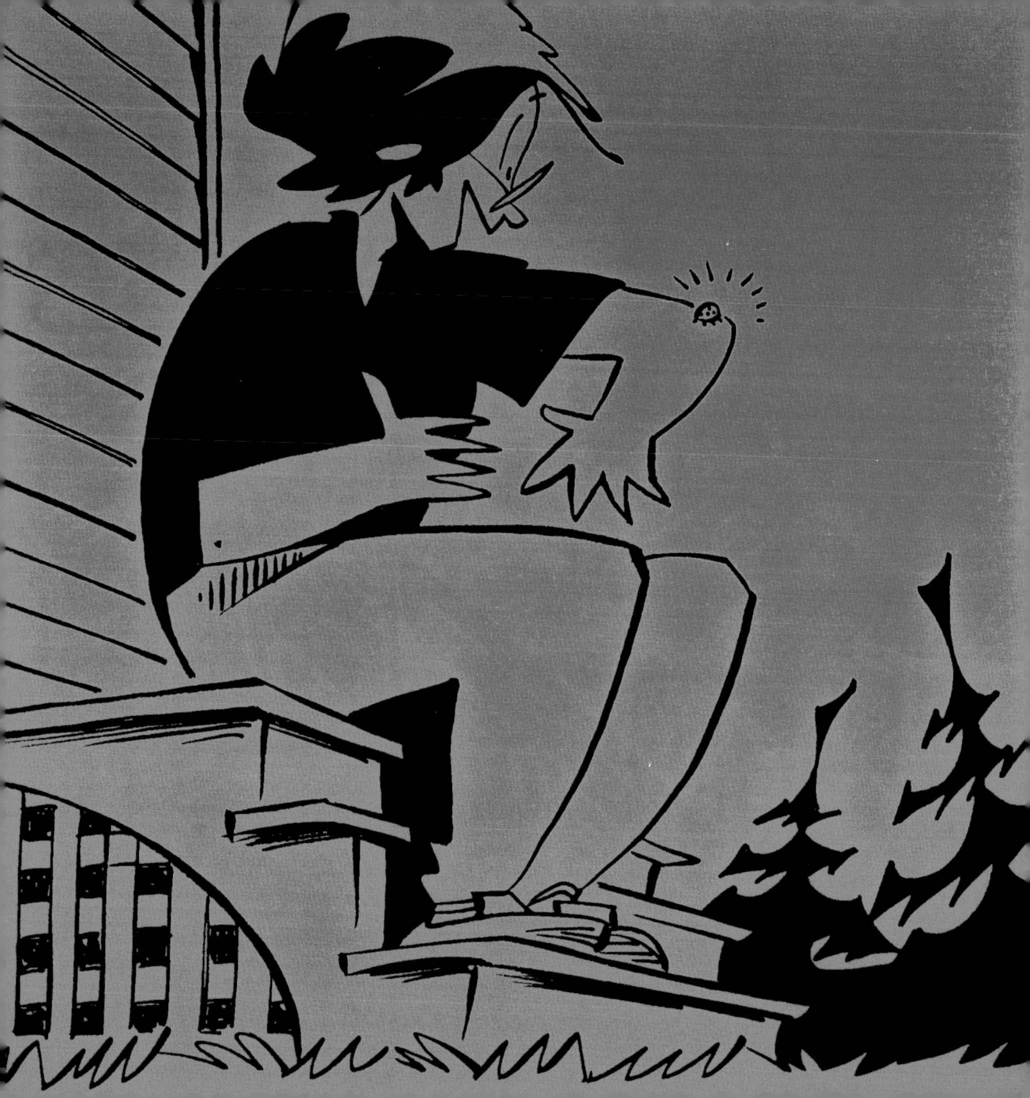

PEACE OF MIND IS A BIG KISS.

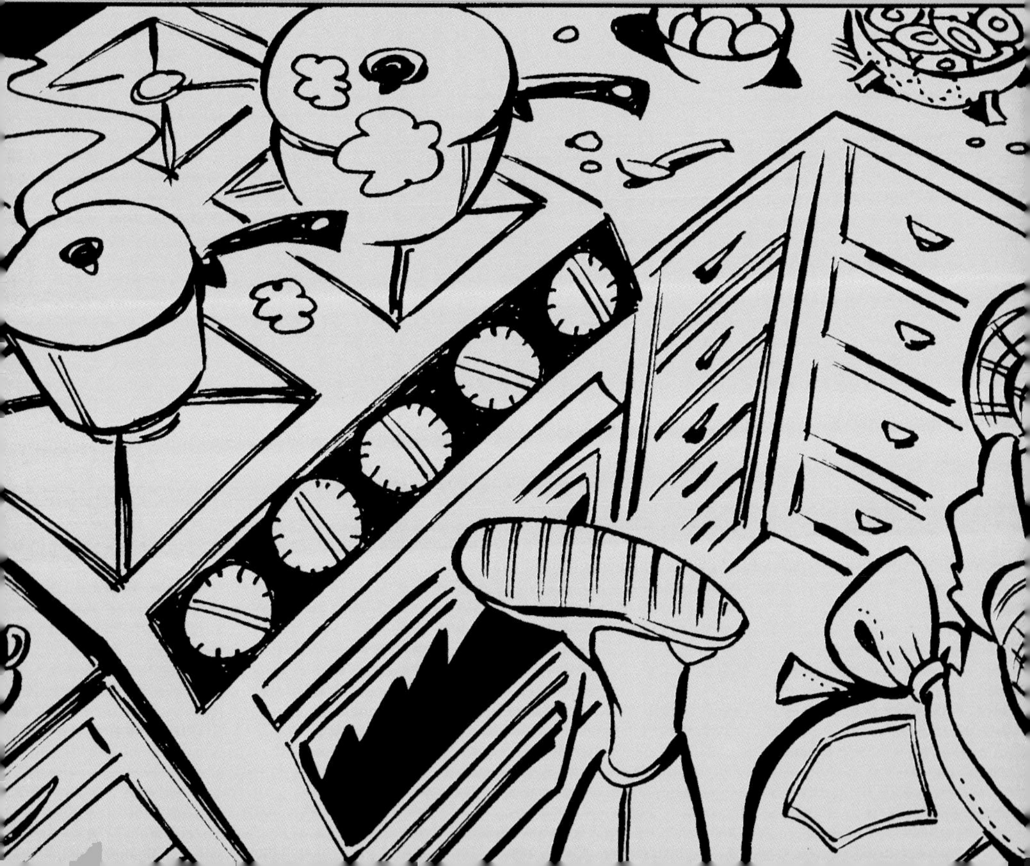

NOT YOURS, THEIRS!

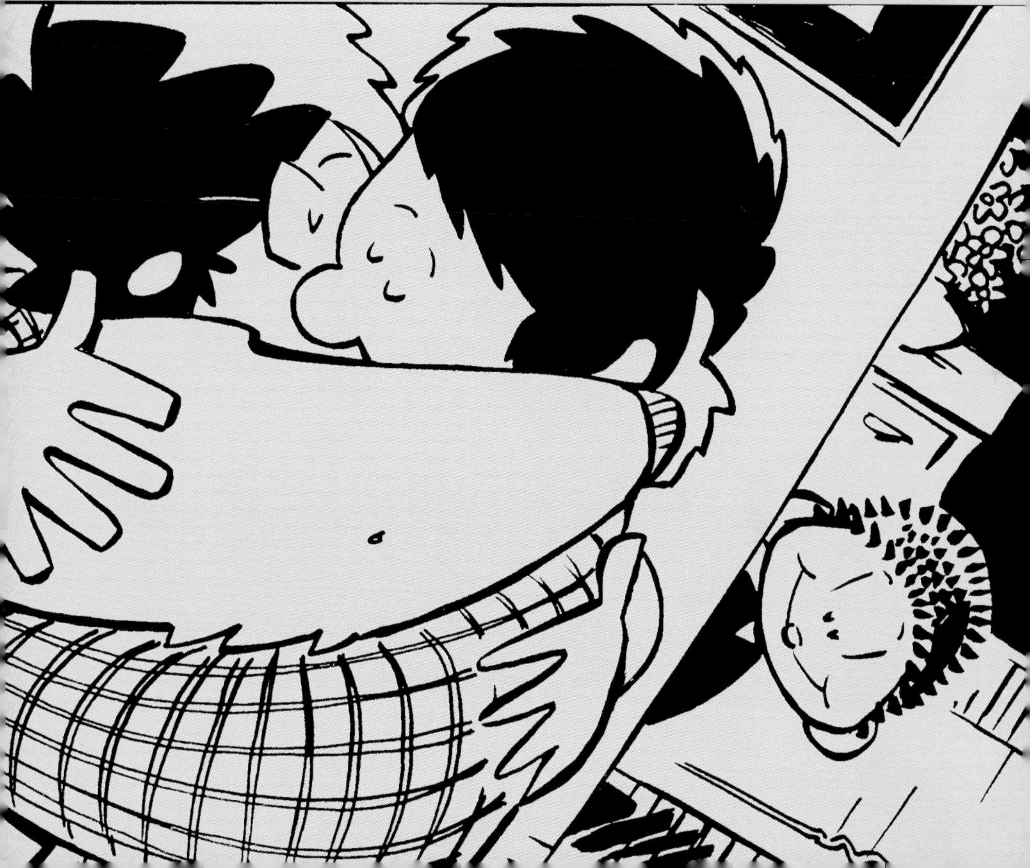

PEACE OF MIND IS NOTICING THE FEMININE TOUCH

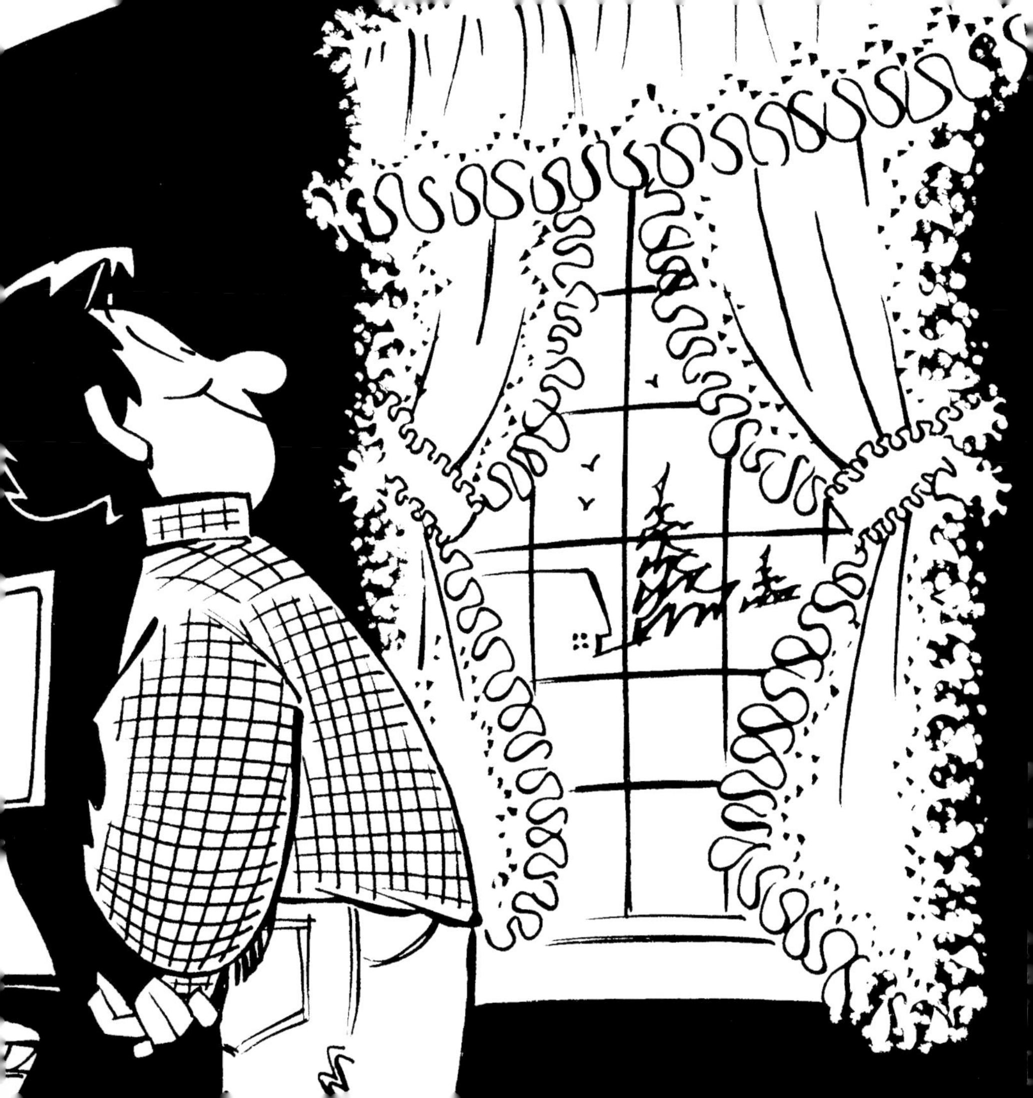

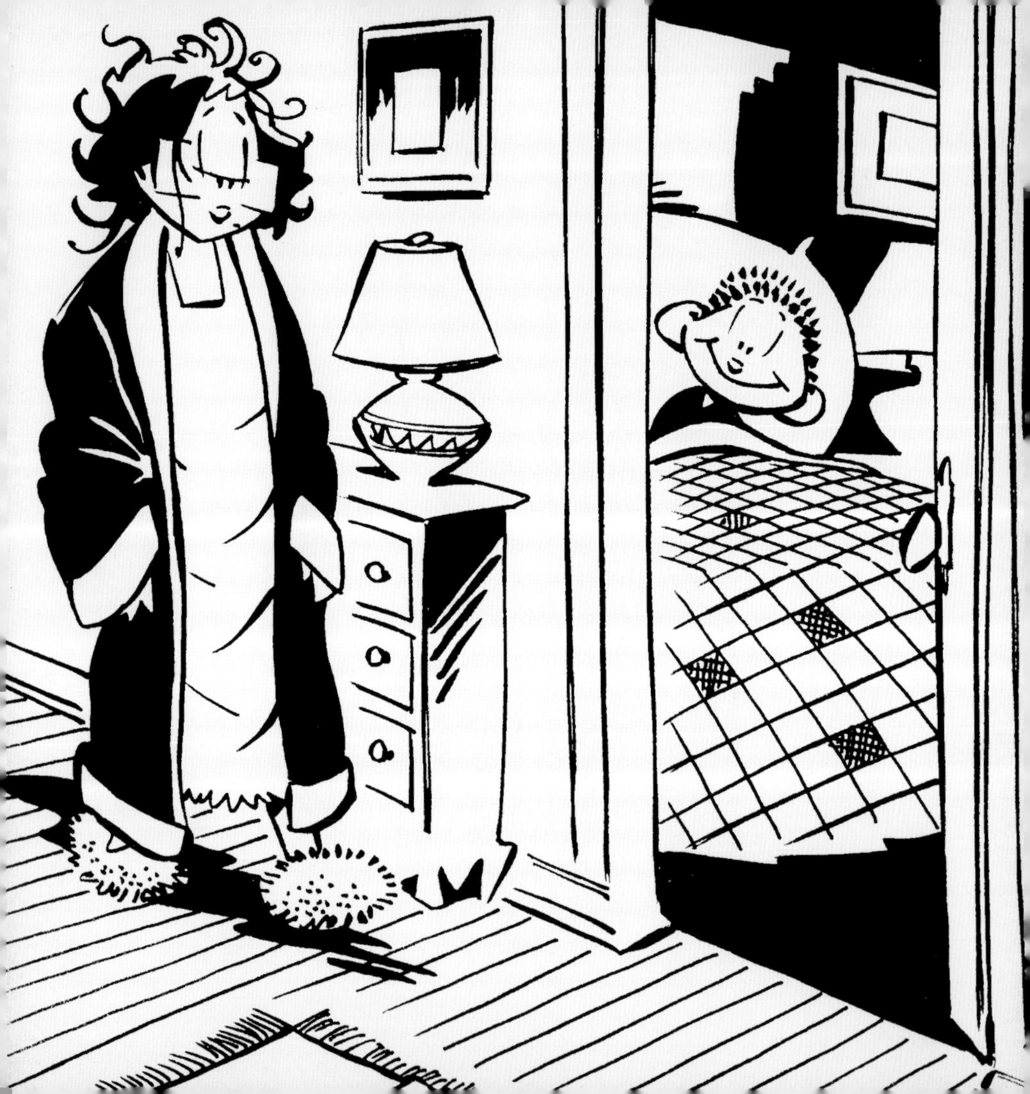

PEACE OF MIND IS SHUFFLING SLIPPERS WHEN YOU CALL YOUR MOMMA AT NIGHT

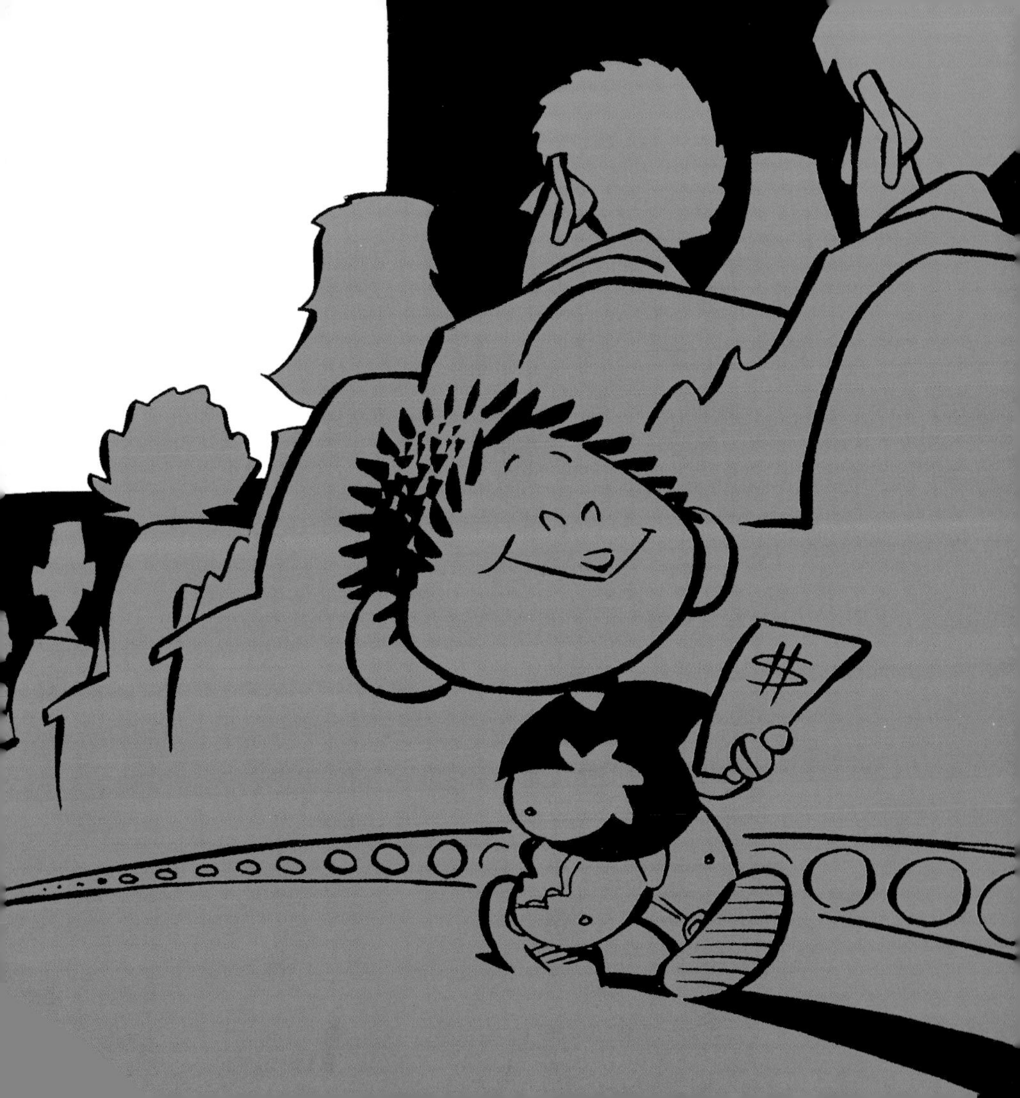
$

PEACE OF MIND IS KNOWING YOU HAVE TIME TO GO TO THE SNACK BAR BEFORE THE MOVIE STARTS

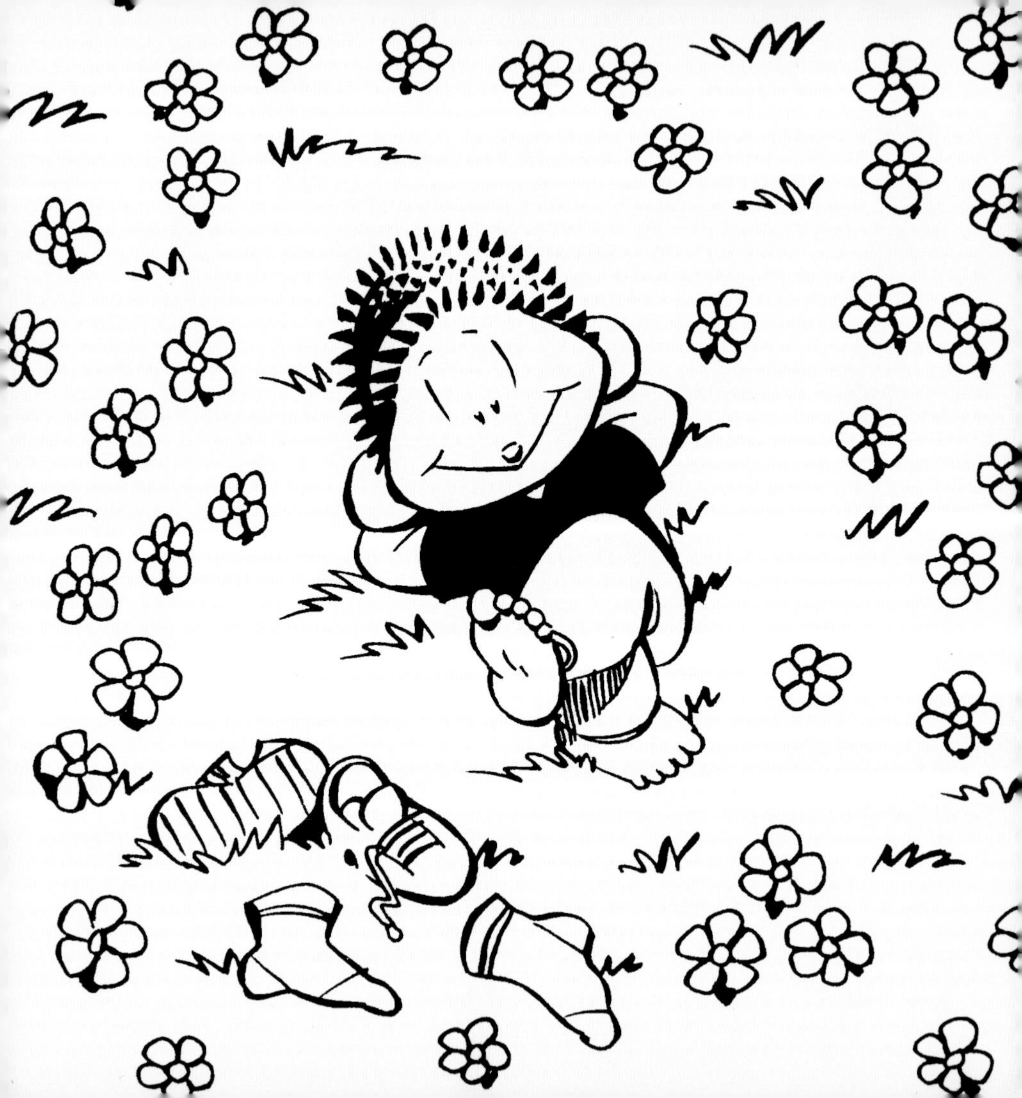

PEACE OF MIND
IS HAVING
NO PLACE SPECIAL TO GO
AND
NOTHING SPECIAL TO DO

PEACE OF MIND IS KNOWING

YOU'LL ALWAYS LAND ON YOUR FEET

PEACE OF MIND IS A HAND STAMP THAT LETS YOU BACK IN FOR FREE

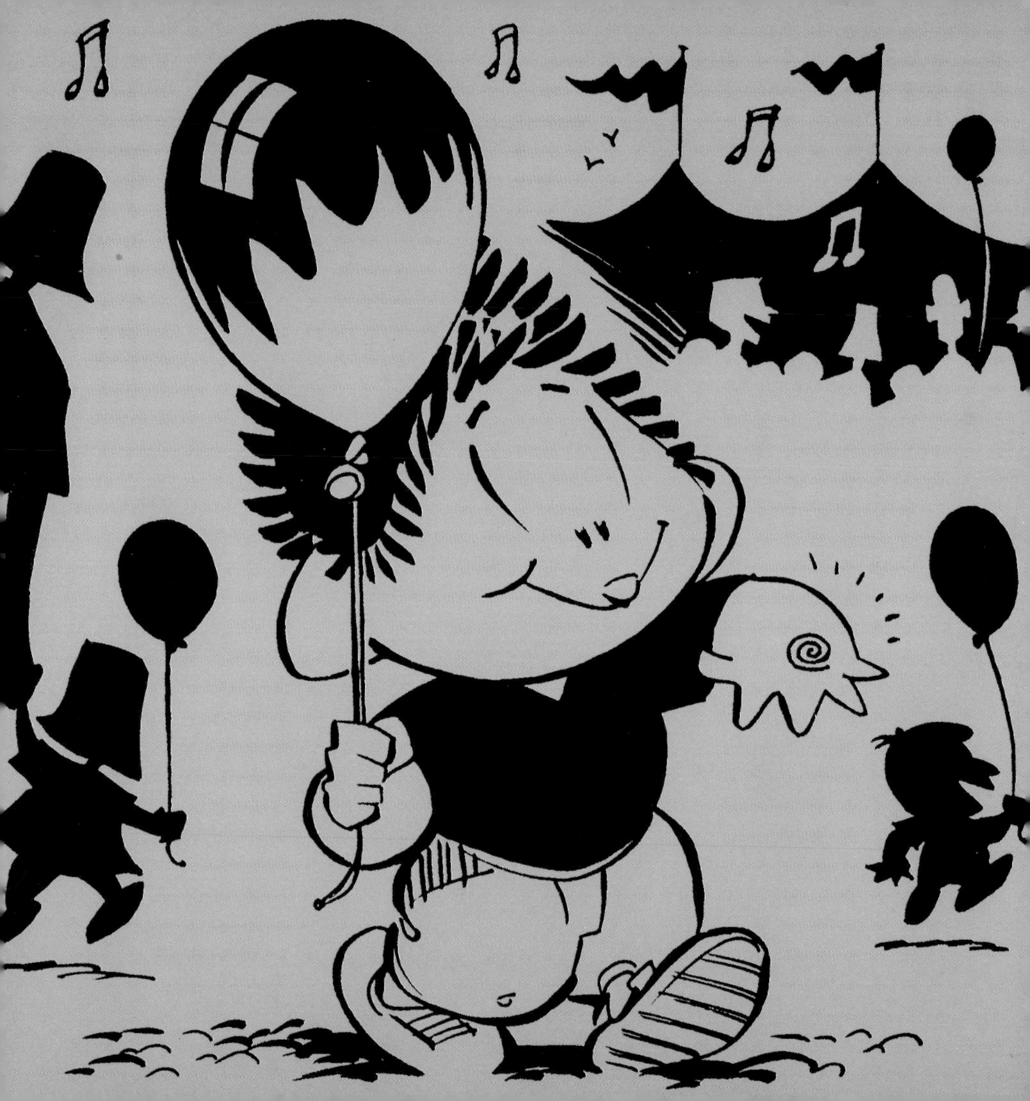

PEACE OF MIND IS FINDING OUT YOUR FRIEND IS IN YOUR CLASS ON THE FIRST DAY OF SCHOOL

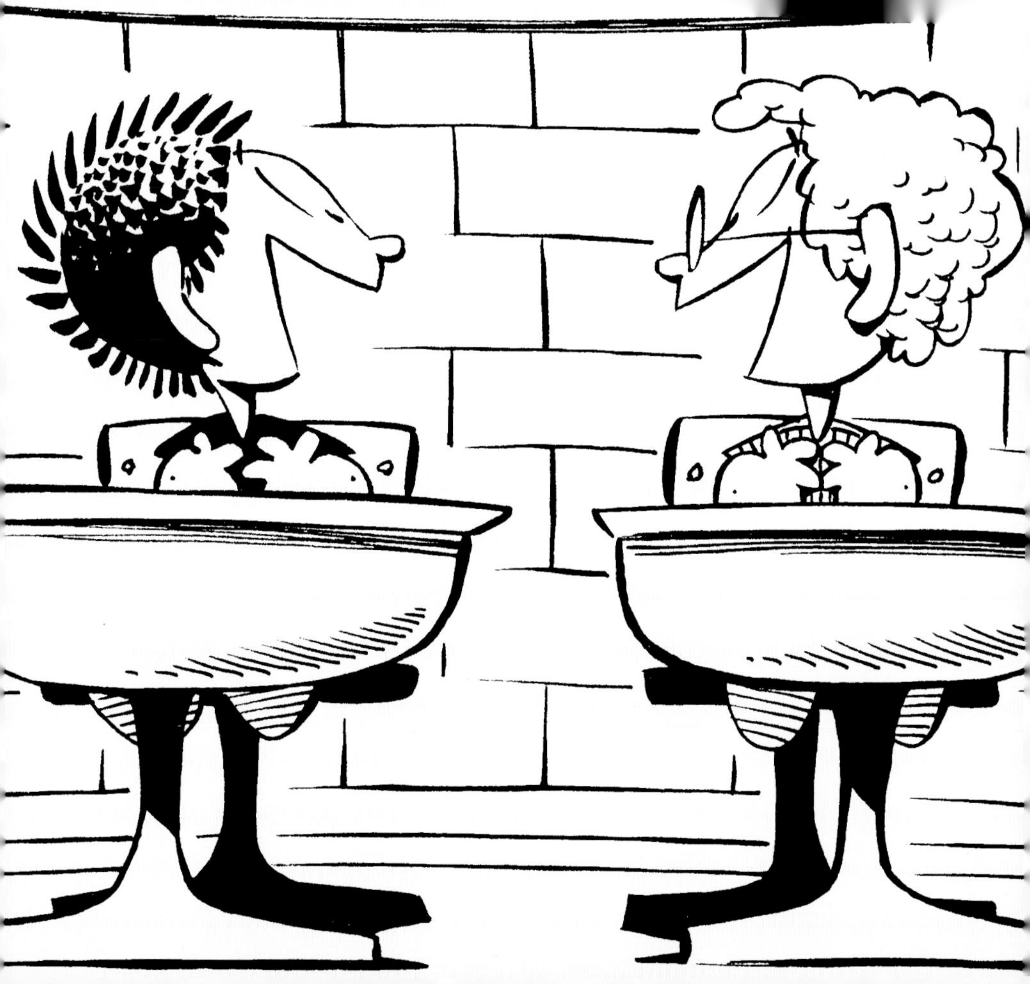

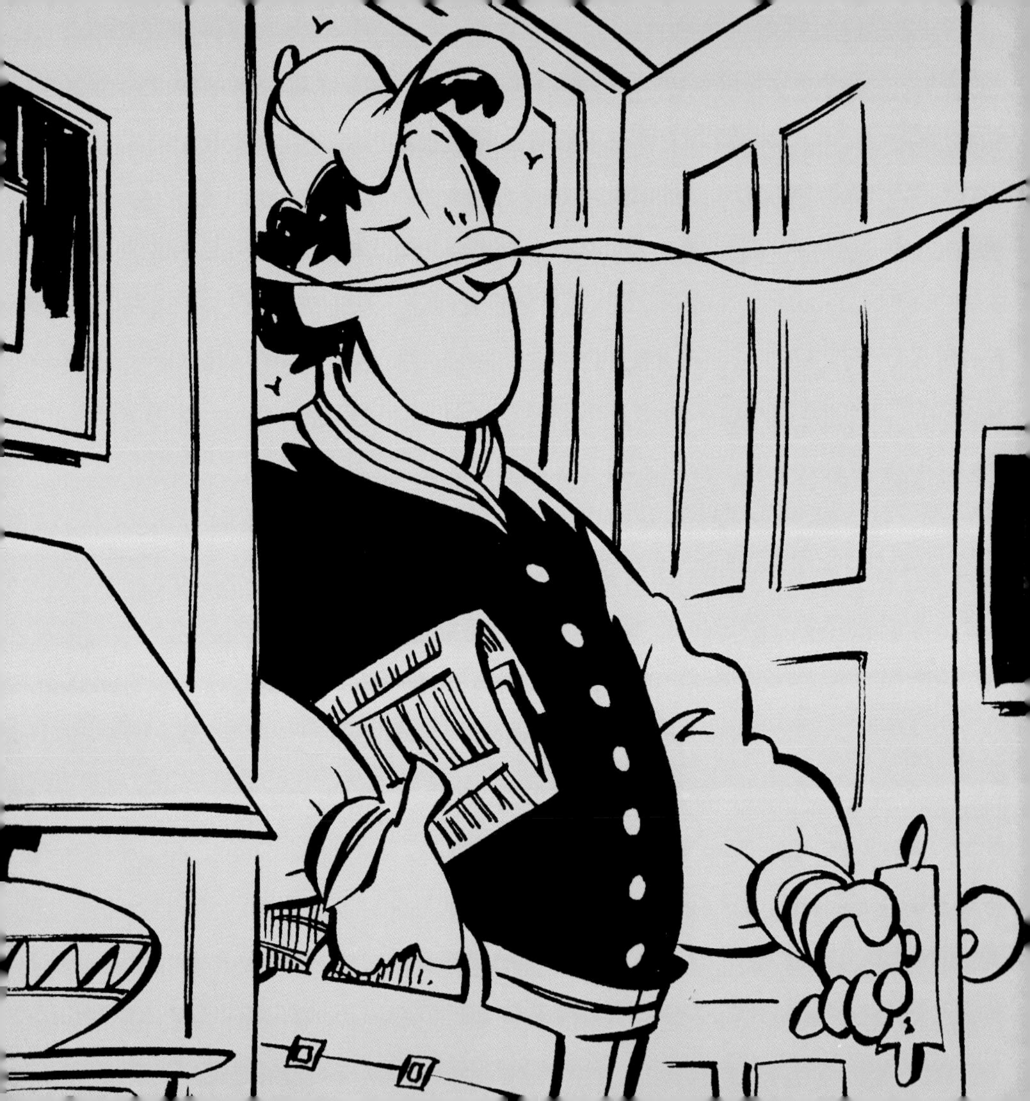

PEACE OF MIND IS THE FIRST WHIFF OF SPAGHETTI SAUCE

PEACE OF MIND IS FEELING YOU'VE

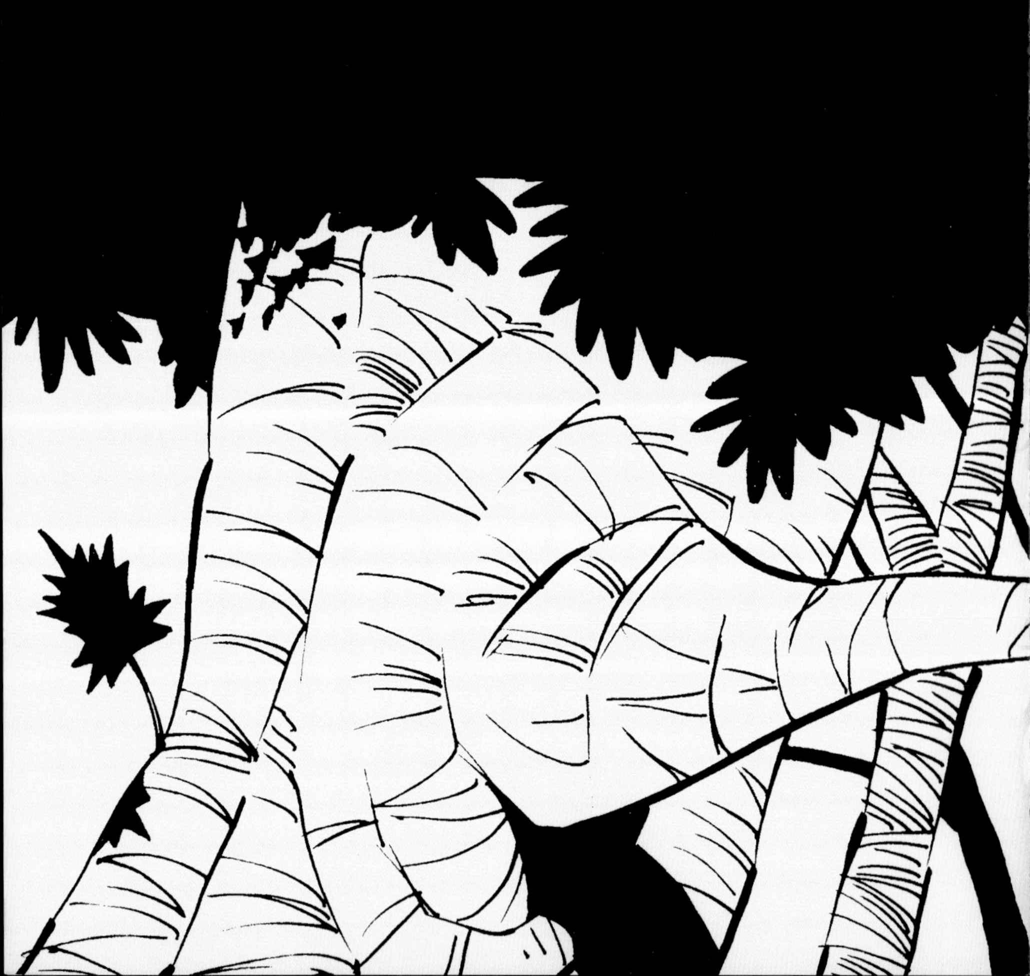

GOT A GOOD GRIP ON LIFE

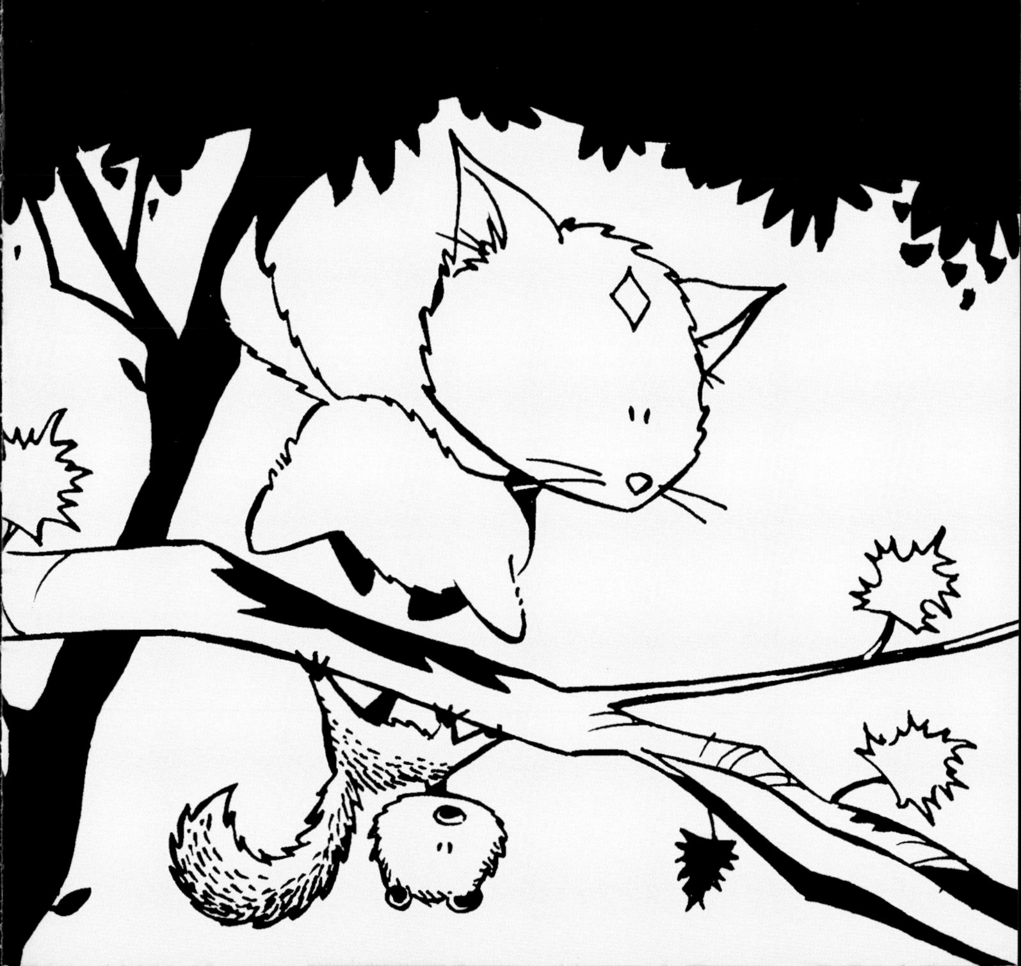

PEACE OF MIND IS
HAVING ALL YOUR
SCHOOL SUPPLIES
READY
THE NIGHT BEFORE

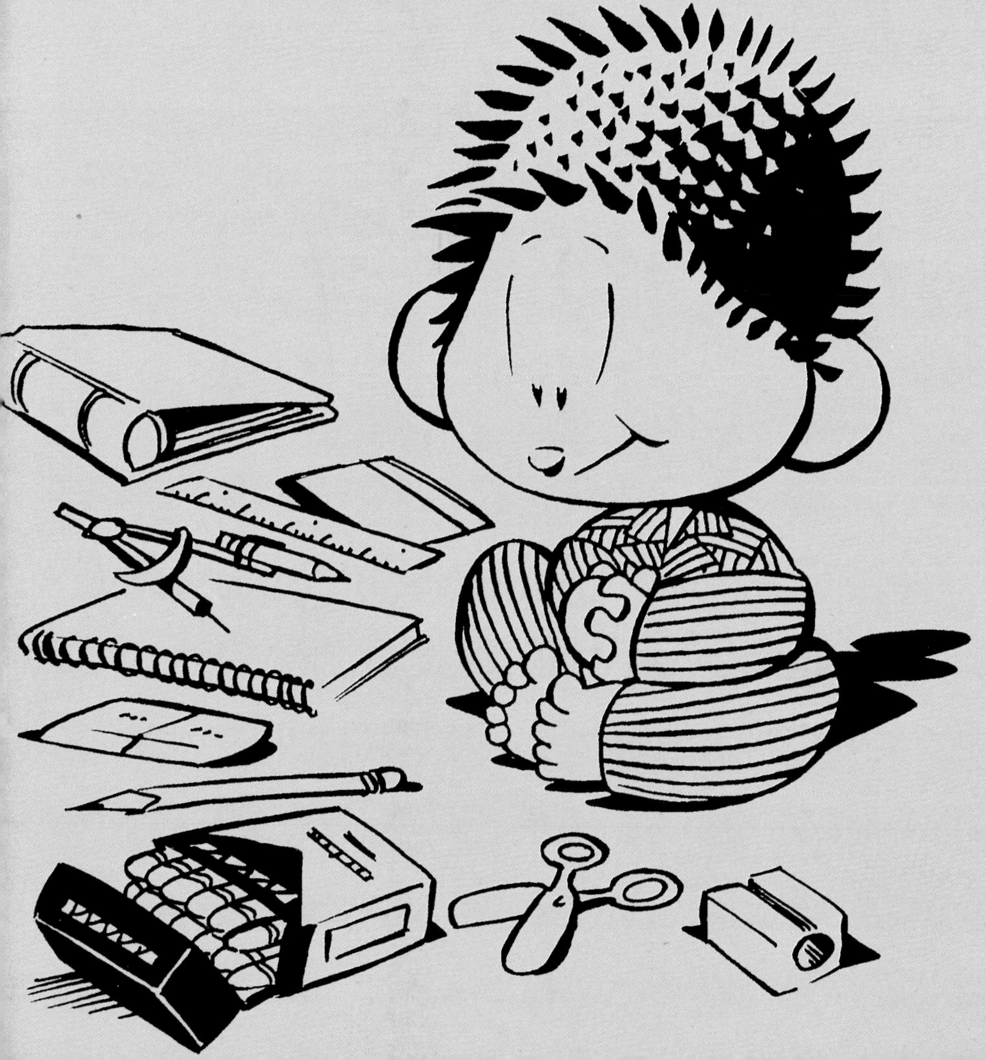

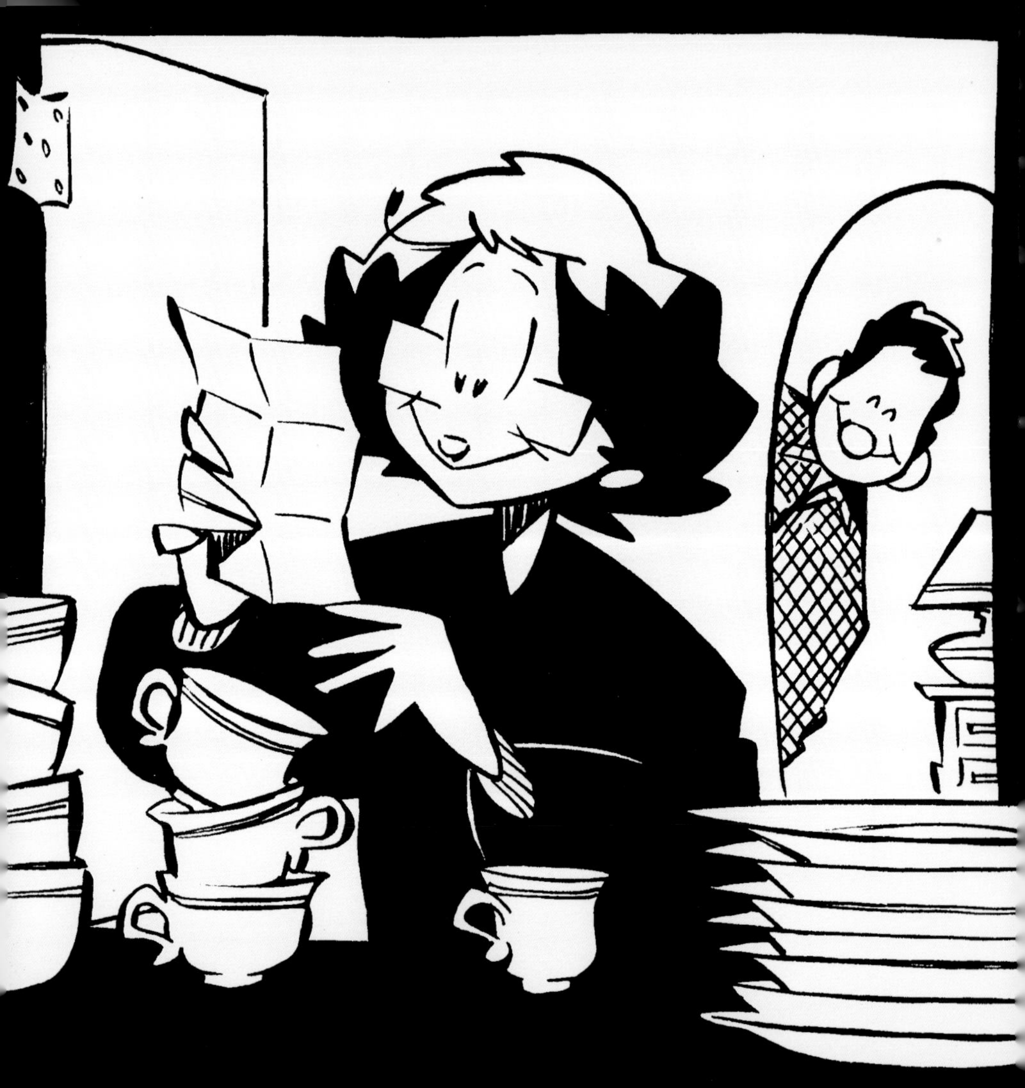

PEACE OF MIND
IS A
LOVE NOTE
IN YOUR
TEA CUP

PEACE OF MIND IS A HOMEMADE RAINBOW

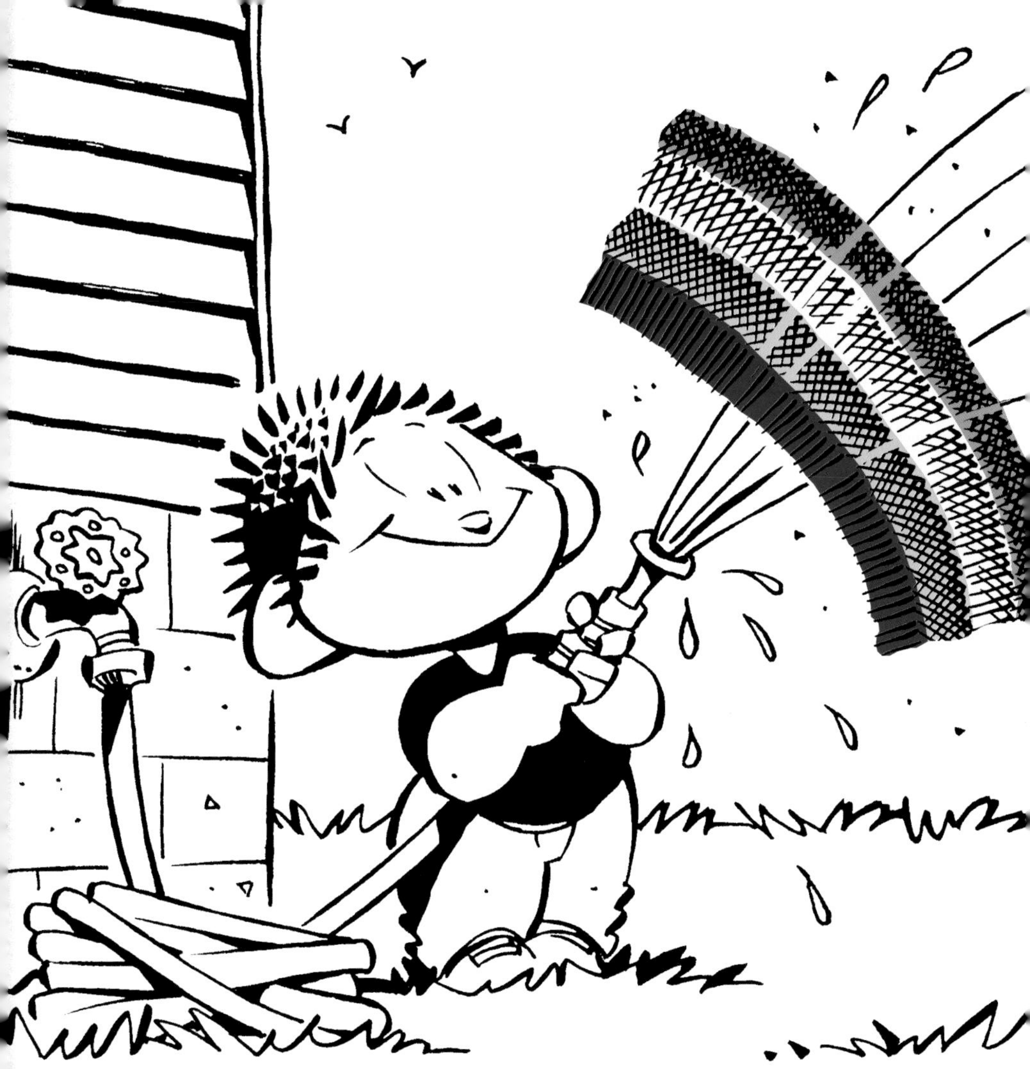

PEACE OF MIND TURNS UP IN THE ODDEST PLACES

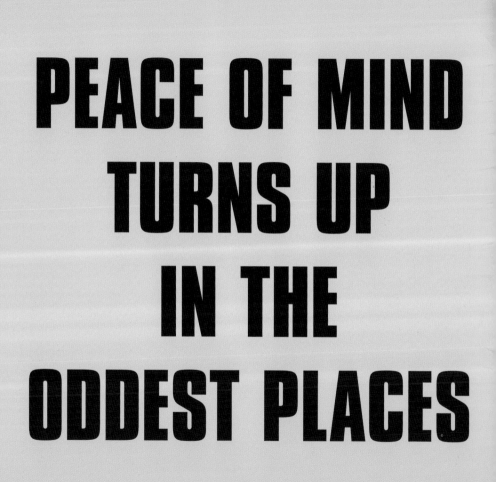

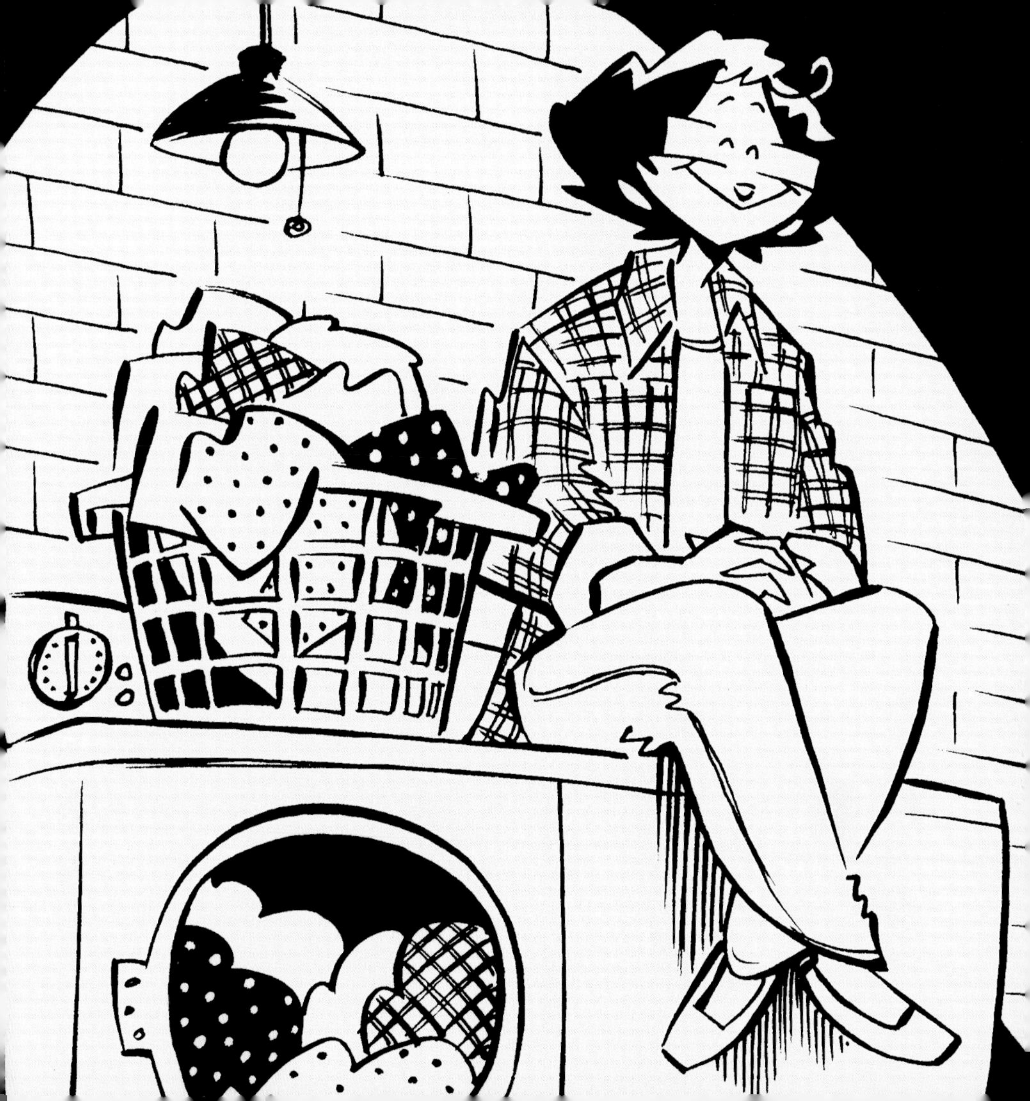

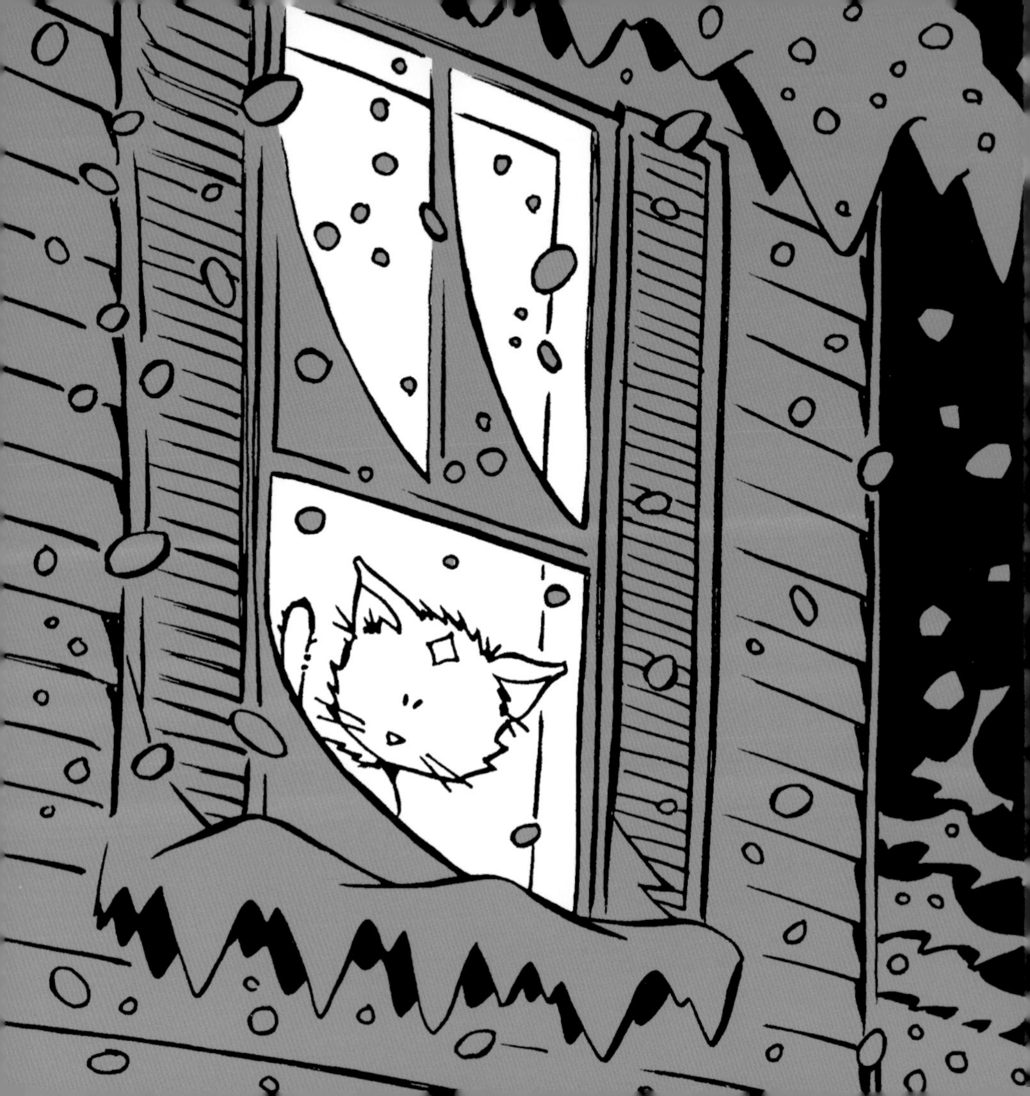

PEACE OF MIND
IS TAKING
A MOMENT
TO COUNT YOUR
BLESSINGS

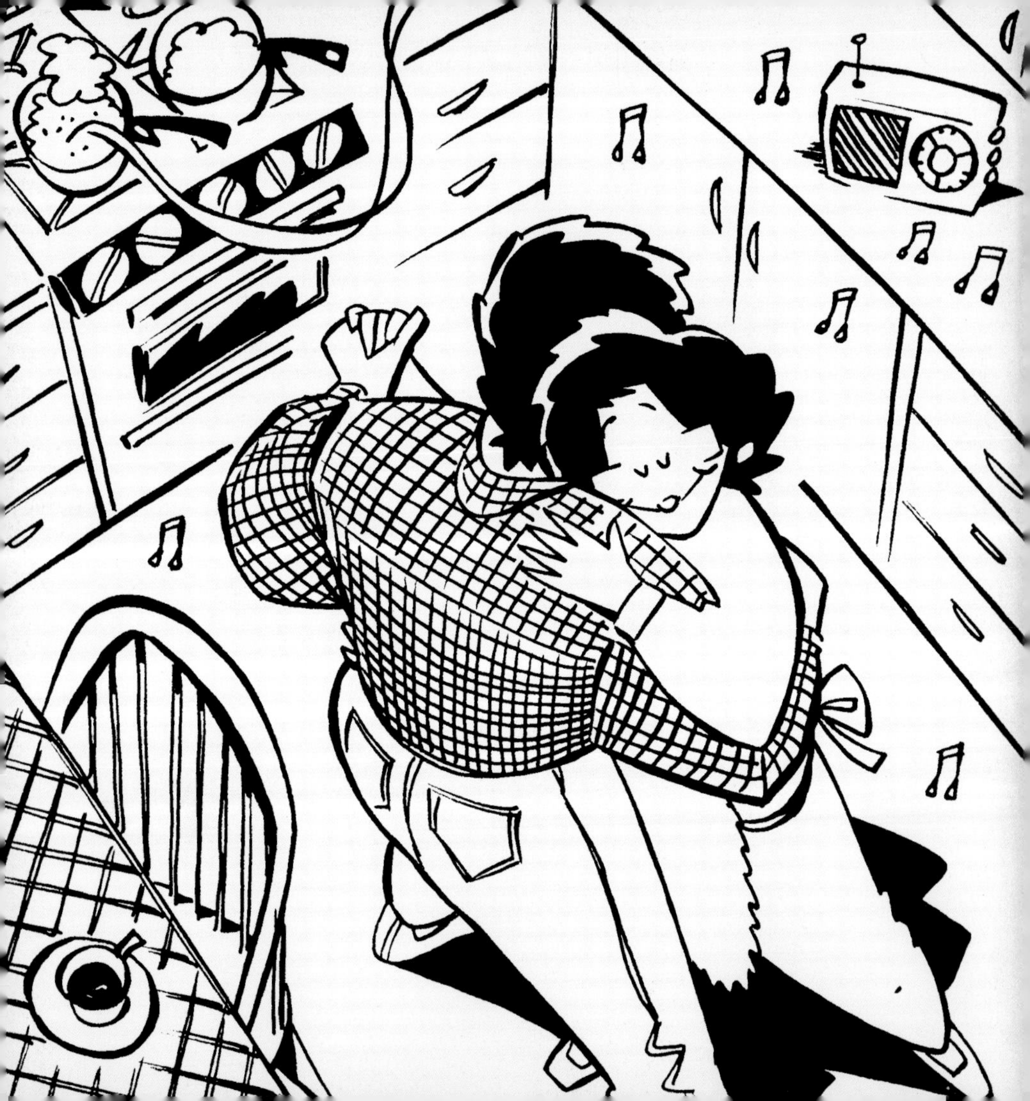

PEACE OF MIND IS A SLOW DANCE IN THE KITCHEN

PEACE OF MIND IS KNOWING YOUR FAVORITE COMIC STRIP WILL BE THERE FOR YOU EVERY DAY

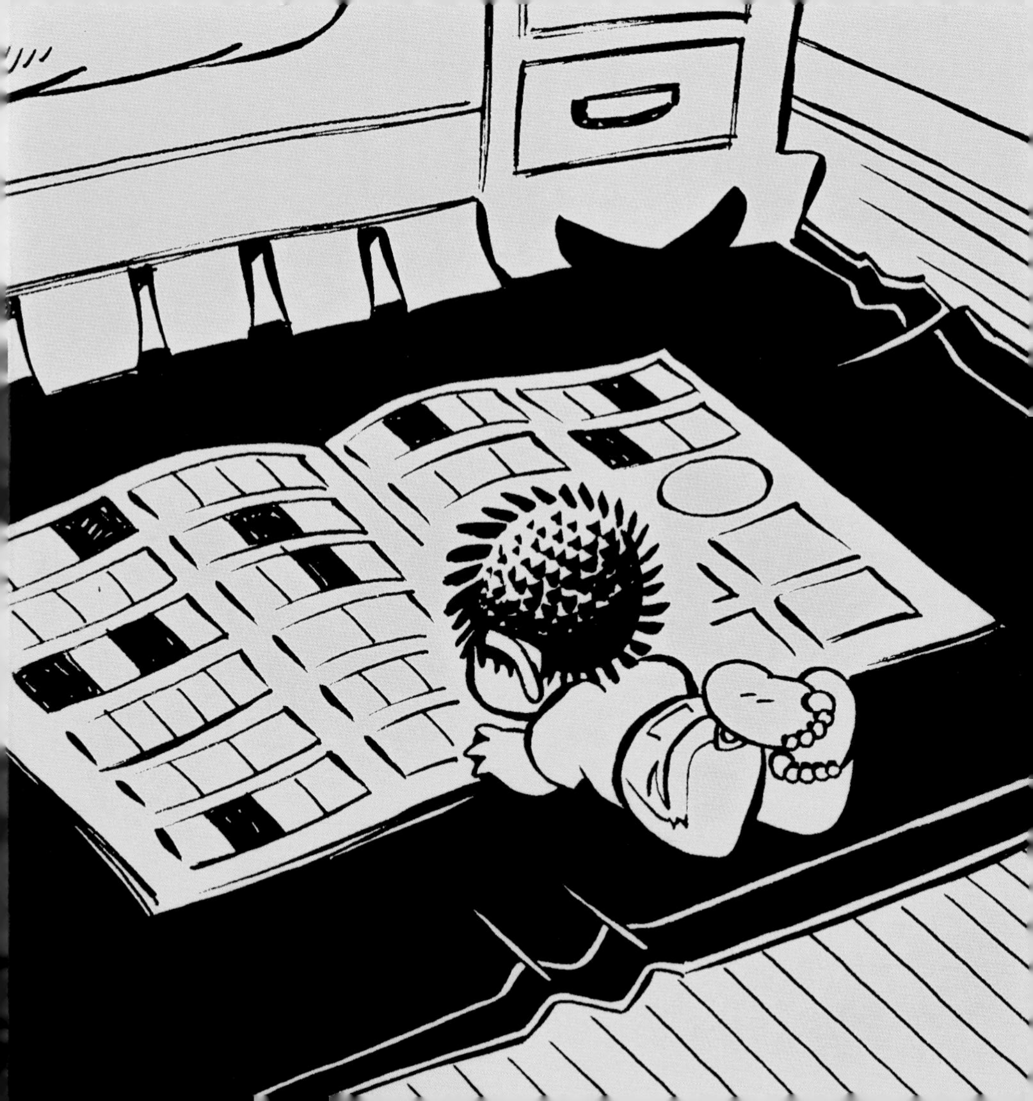

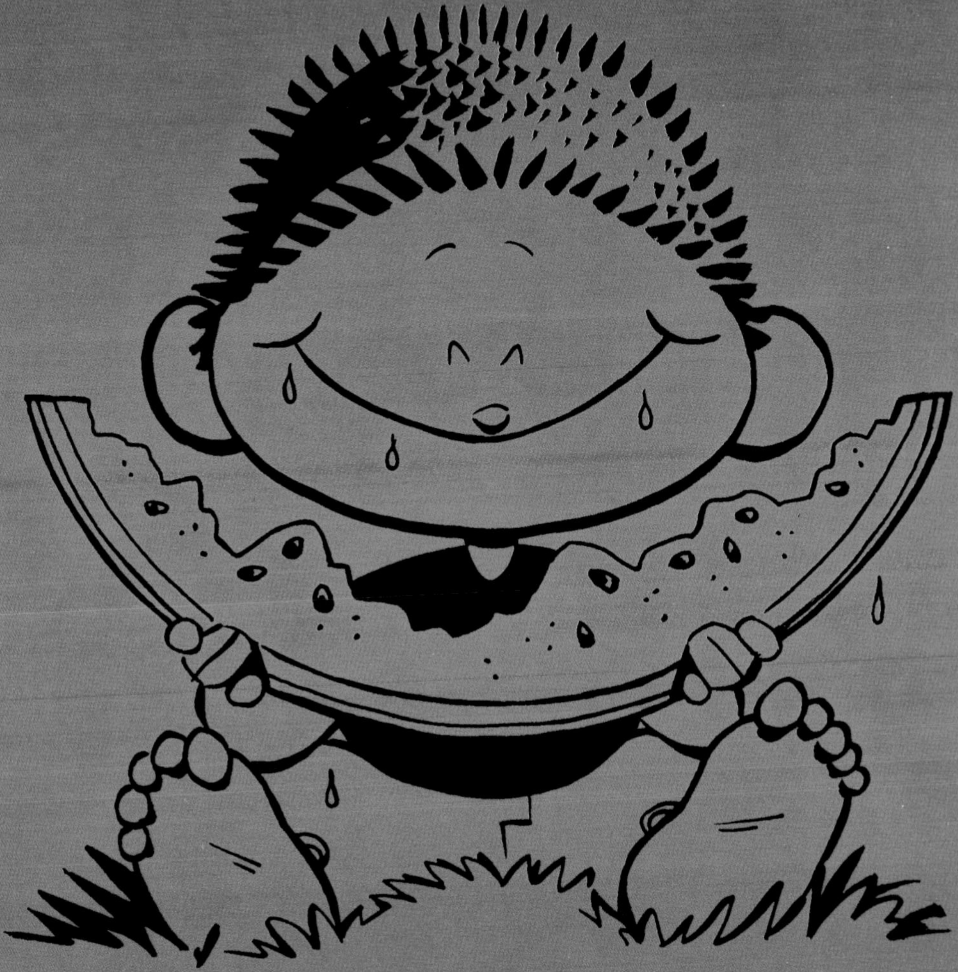

Peace of Mind

is a

Watermelon

Smile

WISHING YOU PEACE OF MIND

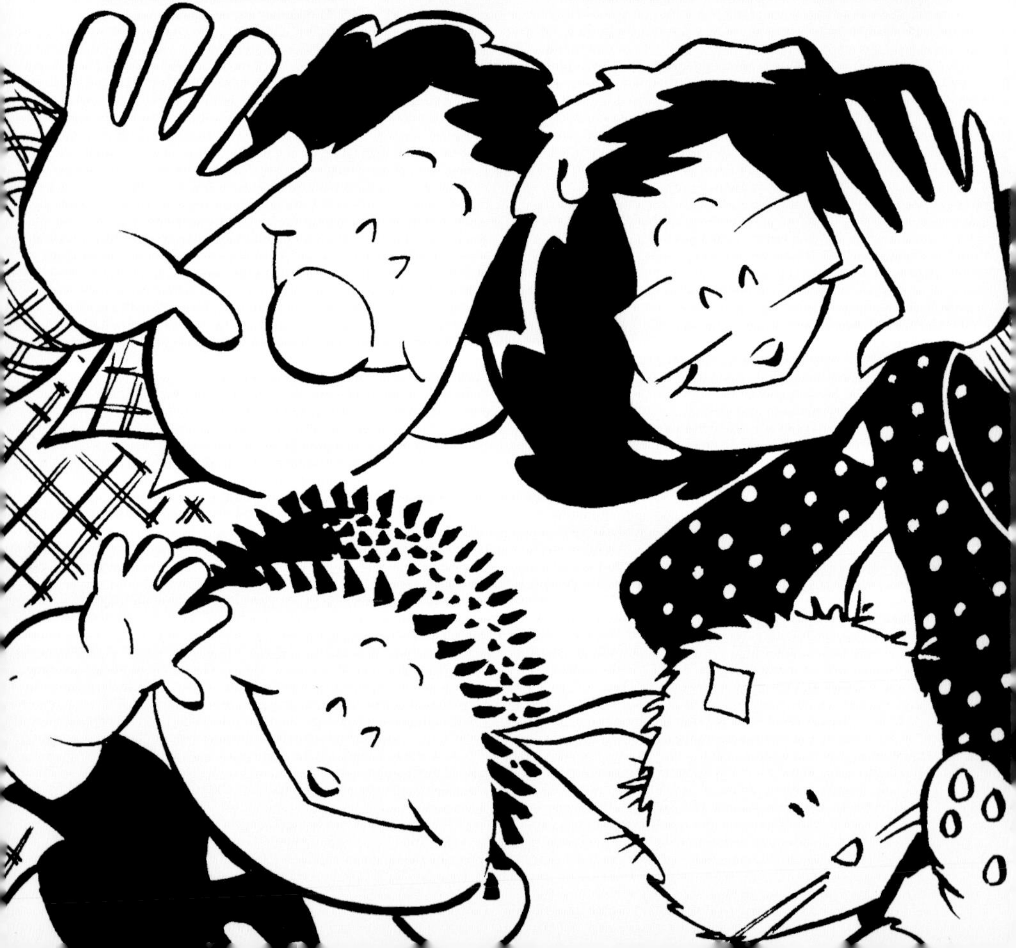